POH BAKES
100 GREATS

POH BAKES
100 GREATS

POH LING YEOW

MURDOCH BOOKS

SYDNEY · LONDON

For my mum, CHRISTINA MEE YOKE YEOW.
Thank you for teaching me to be persistent,
an observer, a stickler for detail.

ANN BENNETT, we miss you.

EMMANUEL MOLLOIS, wherever you are, I hope
there are rivers of chocolate and castles of choux.

TREVOR - hope you are with Zed, floating around
on a cloud in the bluest of skies.

contents

introduction

NOT MANY PEOPLE KNOW THAT MY FIRST LOVE
WAS BAKING, BUT WHEN THE HANDLE ON MY
OVEN DOOR FELL OFF RECENTLY, I TOOK IT AS
A SIGNIFICANT EVENT—METAPHORICALLY
AND FIGURATIVELY.

You see, I *never* seem to have a handle on life and that is one of the main reasons I turn to baking; in short, it chills me right out. Slowing down, having to be precise and concentrate – it's my kind of meditation. I love it so much I've even been known to park myself in front of the oven to watch a cake cook, like television.

When I appeared on the first season of *MasterChef Australia* many moons ago, I was the contestant who often threw herself off high places with my unorthodox takes on Southeast Asian dishes. At the time, it was very much about reclaiming my cultural heritage and nutting out my culinary identity. I had to figure out what I wanted to represent, what I had to offer, that was not necessarily unique, but uniquely me.

After six years of ruminating, I just couldn't run away from the original thought of opening a little cake and pastry shop with my bestie, Sarah – an idea we had when we were in design school. Fast forward 20 years and Jamface was born. First, as a pop-up at the Adelaide Farmers' Market, now also located at the historical Adelaide Central Market, in a cute little cubby house of a shop that my hubby, Jono, and I built. Here, we serve things

that are a wonderful mash-up of French and Australiana – a love child between Paris and the Country Women's Association (CWA), if you will. So this is how the recipes in this book have been informed.

I love being a pragmatic cook – there's far too much out there that is fluff and seduction, but when you crack the goods open, the flavour just isn't there. Since maturing as a cook and running my own joint, I find myself steering further and further away from the notion of plating things up within an inch of their lives. My cakes are the same. They are flavourful, real and uncomplicated. Anything that looks decorative is still there to punch flavour first, looks second.

Going even further back, my love of seeing things rise in the oven started when I was nine, the year we migrated to Australia from Malaysia. My folks were busy assimilating and running their newsagency, so school holidays were strictly an 'amuse yourself' situation. I was never allowed to help much in the kitchen for fear that I would lop off a digit or set myself on fire, but baking was looked upon as an activity that was safe enough. We only ever had meagre pantry basics, so

SIMPLY APPLY THE
FUNDAMENTAL VIRTUES OF
COURAGE, PERSISTENCE AND
STAMINA. I GREW UP SEEING
MUM BAKE THE SAME THING
OVER AND OVER, CRITIQUING
HER OWN WORK HARSHLY:
'HMM, IF I'D ADDED A
TABLESPOON OF CORNFLOUR
IN THAT, IT WOULD HAVE
STABILISED THE MIXTURE MORE',
OR 'HMM, I SHOULD HAVE
KNOWN IT WASN'T QUITE
COOKED BECAUSE IT DIDN'T
SPRING BACK PROPERLY WHEN I
PRESSED THE CENTRE.'

shortbread and sponge cakes were the first things I learned to cook.

On weekends, Mum, who baked fiendishly, took painstaking care training me up on things like how to line a tin meticulously. I remember as if it were yesterday the moment that she taught me the invaluable skill of folding flour into batter, explaining why it had to be done 'just like so'. I used to love seeing her pull out her handwritten recipes in home-ec exercise books she'd trusted since she was a teenager. The pages were brown from age and fragile from good use, and I was fascinated that something so unglamorous could contain potions to concoct such wonderful magic. I guess this *is* the thing that's so addictive about baking. You do feel like a magician when, with a bit of chemistry and physics, you can transform eggs,

butter, sugar and flour into such beautiful, delicious things, with infinite variations ...

To finish, my advice on how to be a better baker? Simply apply the fundamental virtues of courage, persistence and stamina. I grew up seeing Mum bake the same thing over and over, critiquing her own work harshly: 'Hmm, if I'd added a tablespoon of cornflour in that, it would have stabilised the mixture more', or 'Hmm, I should have known it wasn't quite cooked because it didn't spring back properly when I pressed the centre.' Be aware that variables can affect the outcome: using a slightly bigger or smaller tin, whether it be an aluminium or non-stick surface, and take into account the inaccuracy of domestic oven temperatures ... no matter how well a recipe is written, it might still take a couple of goes to get it right.

Never be afraid to make mistakes because with them comes an understanding of the science, the ability to redeem potential disasters and the confidence to adjust recipes. For now, I will bid you adieu and good luck. Don't worry, I've made sure to include mostly easy recipes, with a few aspirational 'hair-tearers' for the more ambitious amongst you. Wield that whisk like a fearless warrior and, most importantly, have a blast!

 x

chapter one
SAVOURY STUNNERS

Quickie Mustard Chicken Filo Triangles

You're on your way home from work, exhausted, and the thought of producing dinner for the family just about melts your brain. For those moments, you want your freezer stocked up with things that are plainly yummy – layers of crunchy, buttery pastry filled with creamy chicken and non-exotic vegetables. Just pop them in the oven to crisp up, and serve with a simple salad. The children don't complain; nervous breakdown averted; dinner sorted.

MAKES 10–12

INGREDIENTS

1–2 tablespoons olive oil

1 large onion, cut into 5 mm (¼ inch) dice

1 cooked roast chicken, bones & skin removed, meat shredded

225–300 g (8–10½ oz/1½–2 cups) frozen pea/carrot/corn mix

185 g (6½ oz/¾ cup) sour cream

3 tablespoons seeded mustard, or to taste

Salt & freshly ground black pepper

1 packet (375 g/13 oz) ready-made filo pastry

150 g (5½ oz) butter, melted

METHOD

To make the filling, combine the olive oil and onion in a medium frying pan over medium–high heat. Sauté for 1 minute or until the onion is soft and golden. Set aside to cool.

In a medium mixing bowl, combine the chicken, frozen vegetables, sour cream, mustard and sautéed onion. Mix well, then add salt and pepper to taste.

To assemble the triangles, slice the filo sheets in half lengthways, so that you have two long rectangles. Place about 2 tablespoons of the filling onto the bottom corner of a piece of filo, shaping it into a triangle. Brush the rest of the filo with some of the melted butter, folding or turning the filled portion along the length of the pastry until it's used up and you have a triangular parcel with a wide base. Place this on another sheet of buttered filo, and turn along the length of it again, so that you wind up with a triangle with many layers of filo. Store the triangles in an airtight container or zip-lock plastic bag, keeping them in separate layers with plastic sheets, and freeze. These will keep well in the freezer for up to a month.

To bake, preheat the oven to 190°C (375°F) fan-forced. Arrange the number of filo triangles you need on a lined baking tray. Bake for about 30 minutes until golden brown and the filling has heated through completely. Serve hot.

Smoked Salmon & Zucchini Slice

I really don't care that I'm re-hashing a retro number that everyone grows up eating, because it's so easy and good. I love this for a summer brunch, lunch or dinner. With a light salad, it's a healthy, economical meal that keeps everyone at the dining table happy. If you have some zucchini growing in the garden, this is a perfect way to use them up, and any leftovers make an excellent lunchbox alternative.

FEEDS 4–6

INGREDIENTS

150 g (5½ oz/1 cup) plain
    (all-purpose) flour
1½ teaspoons baking powder
125 ml (4 fl oz/½ cup) vegetable oil
5 large eggs
150 g (5½ oz) smoked salmon OR
    bacon, diced into 1 cm (½ inch)
    pieces
400 g (14 oz/3 cups) zucchini
    (courgettes), unpeeled &
    coarsely grated
1 large brown onion, diced into
    5 mm (¼ inch) pieces
100 g (3½ oz/1 cup) grated gruyère
    OR cheddar cheese
1 handful freshly chopped herbs
    such as parsley, dill OR mint, OR
    a combination is great
Salt & freshly ground black pepper

METHOD

Preheat the oven to 170°C (325°F) fan-forced. Grease a 25 x 20 x 4 cm (10 x 8 x 1½ inch) rectangular baking tin or ovenproof dish.

To make the slice, combine the flour, baking powder, vegetable oil and eggs in a medium mixing bowl, and whisk until smooth. Add the salmon, zucchini, brown onion, cheese and herbs. Season with salt and pepper, and mix until combined.

Pour into the prepared baking tin, and bake for about 35 minutes until golden brown. Slice and serve hot or cold.

Hero No-Knead Crusty Loaf

'Hero' because it's how you will feel when you haul this rustic beauty out of the oven. Every time I make this *New York Times*-inspired recipe, I'm amazed by how technically undemanding it is. The main ingredient is time, but a cast-iron pot with a lid (a ceramic or glass ovenproof dish will also work) is also imperative. The resulting loaf feels somehow ancient and substantial. It has a serious crust, open crumb and a robust bite, with flavour that hints towards a sourdough. You will enjoy making and eating this over and over again.

MAKES 1 LOAF

INGREDIENTS
450 g (1 lb/3 cups) plain (all-purpose) flour + extra, for dusting
¼ teaspoon instant dried yeast
1¼ teaspoons salt
380–400 ml (13–14 fl oz) water
Polenta (coarse cornmeal) OR wheat bran, for dusting

METHOD
Combine the flour, yeast and salt in a medium–large mixing bowl. Mix together the ingredients quickly with your hands, then make a well in the centre and pour in the water. Using a circular motion, bring the ingredients together to form a sticky, wet dough.

Cover the bowl with plastic wrap, and allow the dough to rest in a draught-free spot in the house – and a warm one if possible – for a minimum of 12 hours (but 18 is preferable), or until the surface of the dough is dotted with bubbles. (In winter, I've found this can be up to 20 hours.) If you tilt the bowl, the bubbles will give the dough a stringy appearance.

Flour your work surface well, scrape the dough onto it, sprinkle with a little more flour, then roughly flatten it with your hands. Give it an envelope fold: pull the front and back into the centre, then repeat with the sides. Sprinkle a generous amount of polenta (the size of a dinner plate) in the centre of a clean tea towel. Place the dough on it seam side up, and sprinkle more polenta on top, before loosely folding the sides of the tea towel to cover it completely. Allow the dough to rise for another 2–8 hours (depending on climate) until it doubles in size and does NOT spring back easily when prodded.

When you feel that the dough is close to being fully risen, place a 25–28 cm (10–11 inch) cast-iron (or glass or ceramic) pot and its lid into the oven and preheat to 210°C (410°F) fan-forced for 30 minutes. When ready to bake, remove the pot from the oven – be very careful, as it will be ragingly hot. Uncover the dough, slide your hand under the tea towel and swiftly flip the dough into the pot.

Shimmy the dough a bit, so that it sits in the centre, then cover and bake for 30 minutes. Remove the lid and bake for a further 30 minutes or until beautifully brown. It should look on the flat side and make a crisp, hollow sound as opposed to a dull thud if tapped. Cool for at least 20 minutes on a wire rack before eating. When you cut into it, the crust should be super crunchy, the air bubbles large and the texture a little chewy.

Beef Stout Pie with Blue Cheese Crust

I always feel really sorry for British food because it often cops such a brutal bagging. If you're one of those cynics, this will seriously shut you up – a rich, crumbly blue cheese pastry, filled with the most luscious pull-apart beef that has been stewing in wonderfully English things such as stout and worcestershire sauce.

FEEDS 8–10

PASTRY
170 g (6 oz) Stilton cheese OR any other strong blue cheese, crumbled
400 g (14 oz/2⅔ cups) plain (all-purpose) flour + extra, for dusting
50 g (1¾ oz) chilled unsalted butter, diced
40 g (1½ oz) Copha (white vegetable shortening) OR any vegetable shortening, coarsely grated
125 ml (4 fl oz/½ cup) iced water
1 egg, lightly whisked, for egg wash

FILLING
Olive oil
2 kg (4 lb 8 oz) beef cheeks OR chuck (braising) steak, cut into thick steaks
Salt & freshly ground black pepper
50 g (1¾ oz) butter
3 garlic cloves, finely chopped
3 large brown onions, 1 roughly chopped, 2 thinly sliced
3 carrots, coarsely chopped
2 celery stalks, coarsely chopped

METHOD
To make the pastry, combine the Stilton, flour, butter and Copha in a food processor and pulse into pea-size crumbs. Gradually add the water and pulse until the dough starts to gather into a single mass. Shape the dough into a disc, and cover in plastic wrap. Rest in the refrigerator for 30 minutes.

Pour a good dash of olive oil into a large stainless-steel frying pan, and brown the beef well over high heat. Make sure that you do this in batches, so that you don't overcrowd the pan. Season both sides of the meat with salt and pepper as you go. Transfer the caramelised beef to a plate. Set aside.

Combine the butter, a dash of olive oil, garlic, the chopped onion, carrots and celery in the same pan, and sauté over medium heat until soft but not coloured. Add the beer, stock and bouquet garni. Simmer until the liquid has reduced by one-third. Return the beef to the pan, cover and simmer over medium–low heat until the beef is tender enough that it pulls apart easily. Transfer the beef to a cutting board (reserve the braising liquid in the pan), then use two forks to shred the meat roughly. Set aside.

In a medium non-stick frying pan, cook the sliced onions over medium heat until well caramelised – dark brown with a little charring; take your time with this step. Add to the saucepan of reserved braising liquid, together with the worcestershire sauce, port and sugar. Bring to the boil, reduce the heat and simmer for 10 minutes, then return the shredded beef to the saucepan.

To make the beurre manié, on a small plate, press the butter and flour together with a fork, to form a smooth paste. Add enough of this to thicken the filling to your liking. Spread the filling over a baking tray, cover loosely with plastic wrap and cool, then chill completely.

Meanwhile, preheat the oven to 170°C (325°F) fan-forced, and have a 22 x 5 cm (8½ x 2 inch) round pie dish on stand-by.

To assemble the pie, divide the dough into two even pieces. Cut a quarter chunk out of one, and add it to the other so that one is now slightly larger, then form them into two discs. Cover in plastic wrap, and rest in the refrigerator for 15 minutes.

Lightly flour your work surface, and roll out the larger disc into a circle 37 cm (14½ inches) in diameter and 4 mm (³/₁₆ inch) thick. Use it to line the pie dish; trim off any excess pastry, but leave enough so that there is a 2 cm (¾ inch) overhang around the edges. Add the trimmings to the remaining disc of pastry, and roll out to a 4 mm (³/₁₆ inch) thick circle. Cut out a 2 cm (¾ inch) hole at the centre – this allows any excess steam to escape.

Fill the pie with the chilled filling, then gently drape the pastry lid over the top. Trim the top layer of pastry to roughly match the bottom one, then crimp or pleat the edges attractively to seal. If you like, you can cut some leaf shapes with any remaining pastry to decorate the pie. To finish, baste the pie generously with egg wash.

Bake for about 1 hour until the pastry crust is dark golden. Remove from the oven, and leave to rest for 10–15 minutes before serving.

750 ml (26 fl oz/3 cups) stout
   OR dark ale
500 ml (17 fl oz/2 cups) beef stock
Bouquet garni (made up of 2 bay
   leaves, 1 sprig of rosemary,
   10 sprigs of thyme & 4 stalks
   of parsley, tied together with
   kitchen string)
2 tablespoons worcestershire sauce
2 tablespoons port OR Pedro
   Ximénez sherry
2 teaspoons sugar

BEURRE MANIÉ
50 g (1¾ oz) butter
35 g (1¼ oz/¼ cup) plain
   (all-purpose) flour

BEEF STOUT PIE WITH
BLUE CHEESE CRUST

PIZZA RUSTICA

Pizza Rustica

Imagine all the Italian ingredients we know and love – sausage, ham, spinach, ricotta, mozzarella and parmesan – bunged in a pie. Delicious and light; perfect with a salad. This also slices and keeps its shape very well – perfect for a lunchbox or picnic.

FEEDS ABOUT 10

PASTRY

200 g (7 oz) chilled unsalted butter, diced into 2 cm (¾ inch) pieces
390 g (13¾ oz) plain (all-purpose) flour + extra, for dusting
1½ tablespoons caster (superfine) sugar
1½ teaspoons salt
1 egg + 1 extra egg yolk
70 ml (2¼ fl oz) iced water

FILLING

3 tablespoons olive oil
250 g (9 oz) fresh medium–hot Italian sausages, casings removed
2 garlic cloves, finely chopped
1 large bunch (about 600–700 g/ 1 lb 5 oz–1 lb 9 oz) silverbeet (Swiss chard) OR English spinach with stalks, finely chopped OR 285 g (10 oz) chopped frozen spinach
120 g (4¼ oz) thinly sliced prosciutto, cut into 2 cm (¾ inch) pieces
2 eggs, whisked

METHOD

To make the pastry, combine the butter, flour, sugar and salt in a food processor and pulse until you have a sandy mixture. Add the egg, yolk and water, and pulse until the mixture begins to form a single mass. At this point, tip the mixture into a large mixing bowl – a good amount should still be a crumbly mess. Instead of kneading, use a squeezing action to bind the rest of the crumbs together to form a fat sausage. Divide the dough into two even pieces. Cut a one-third chunk out of one, and add it to the other, then shape them into discs. Cover both with plastic wrap, and rest in the refrigerator for 20 minutes.

Meanwhile, make the filling. Heat 1 tablespoon of the olive oil with the Italian sausage meat in a medium non-stick frying pan over low heat to render out some of the fat. Increase to medium–high heat and brown the meat, breaking up any large chunks as you go. Add the garlic and sauté until fragrant but not coloured. Transfer to a plate to cool completely before using.

Heat the remaining olive oil in the same frying pan over medium heat. Add the silverbeet, and cook until all the moisture from the leaves has evaporated. Transfer to a colander, and allow to drain. Cool completely, then squeeze out any excess moisture.

Combine the prosciutto, eggs, ricotta, mozzarella, parmesan, parsley, cooled sausage mixture and wilted silverbeet in a large mixing bowl. Add pepper to taste. Fold gently to combine, or mix with clean hands.

Preheat the oven to 200°C (400°F) fan-forced. Have a 24–26 cm (9½–10½ inch) springform tin on stand-by.

On a lightly floured work surface, roll out each disc of pastry into circles 3–4 mm (⅛–³⁄₁₆ inch) thick. The larger one should be enough to line the bottom and side of the springform tin, but still have about 2 cm (¾ inch) of overhang. Sprinkle the bottom of the pastry with the breadcrumbs (to soak up any excess moisture), then top up with the cooled filling. Carefully place the smaller circle of pastry on top, then crimp or fold the edges over to seal the pie. Brush the top lavishly with the egg wash, sprinkle with a little extra parmesan, then use a paring knife to stab a few holes into the lid to allow the steam to escape.

Bake for 10 minutes, then reduce the heat to 180°C (350°F) fan-forced and bake for a further 45 minutes until beautifully golden on top. Allow to rest for 30 minutes before serving.

300 g (10½ oz/1⅓ cups) low-fat ricotta cheese
200 g (7 oz/1½ cups) shredded mozzarella cheese
35 g (1¼ oz/⅓ cup) parmesan OR pecorino cheese, freshly grated + 1 tablespoon for sprinkling
1 scant cup roughly chopped flat-leaf (Italian) parsley
Freshly ground black pepper

BITS & PIECES
1–1½ tablespoons dried breadcrumbs
1 egg, whisked, for egg wash

Salmon, Mussel & Cider Pie

This is inspired by an old Gary Rhodes recipe I've made many times over the years. It's such a lovely, comforting way to eat seafood, in a pie, but we don't seem to do it much here in Australia. This is a wonderful dish to make for dinner parties because it's old-school sophistication and comfort all in one.

FEEDS 4

INGREDIENTS

400 g (14 oz) salmon fillets OR any
    firm-fleshed white fish, skin off
½ quantity Rough Puff Pastry
    (see page 200)
25 g (1 oz) butter
4 leeks, halved lengthways, sliced
    5 mm (¼ inch) thick
1 large handful flat-leaf (Italian)
    parsley, roughly chopped

MUSSELS

2 kg (4 lb 8 oz) black mussels,
    debearded & cleaned
25 g (1 oz) butter
2 brown onions, sliced
3 garlic cloves, sliced
12 sprigs of thyme
600 ml (21 fl oz) cider, beer
    OR dry white wine
1 litre (35 fl oz/4 cups) water

ROUX

50 g (1¾ oz) butter
75 g (2½ oz/½ cup) plain
    (all-purpose) flour
170 ml (5½ fl oz/⅔ cup) thin
    (pouring) cream
Finely grated zest & juice of 1 lemon
Salt & freshly ground black
    pepper

METHOD

To prepare the mussels, melt the butter in a large saucepan over medium heat. Add the onions, garlic and thyme, and sweat until fragrant but not coloured. Pour in the cider and water, and bring to the boil, then add the mussels and cover. When the mussels have opened, remove all the cooked flesh and discard the shells. Place the mussel meat in a bowl, and ladle some of the cooking liquid over the top to keep it moist. Set aside.

Strain the stock through a fine-meshed sieve to catch any shell or grit, then return it to the saucepan. Simmer until reduced in volume by one-quarter. Set aside.

Preheat the oven to 200°C (400°F) fan-forced.

To cook the fish, place the fillets in an ovenproof dish with 125 ml (4 fl oz/½ cup) of the mussel stock, and cover with foil. Bake for about 5 minutes until the salmon is ever so slightly pink in the middle. Flake the fish into large pieces. Set aside.

Turn the oven down to 190°C (375°F) fan-forced. Roll out the puff on a lightly floured work surface until 5 mm (¼ inch) thick, then cut into four 10 cm (4 inch) circles with a pastry cutter. Place these on a tray lined with baking paper, and bake for about 25 minutes or until a deep golden brown. Remove from the oven and set aside.

To make the roux, melt the butter in a medium non-stick saucepan over medium heat. Add the flour, stirring vigorously with a wooden spoon, and cook for about 4 minutes or until a pale brown colour. Add the stock one ladle at a time, whisking until well combined before adding more. Repeat until all the stock is used up. Add the cream, and whisk to combine, then mix in the lemon zest and juice. Add salt and pepper to taste.

To start pulling it all together, pop the puff pastry circles in a 100°C (200°F) fan-forced oven to reheat. Meanwhile, melt the remaining 25 g (1 oz) butter in a medium saucepan over medium heat. Add the leeks and cook until soft. Add the parsley, mussels, flaked salmon and half of the roux mixture, then very gently fold it together. If you feel the mixture needs more sauce, fold in more roux.

To serve, spoon the mixture into four dishes, and top with the pastry.

Baked Camembert with Thyme, Garlic & Red Wine

If you are having a winter dinner party and would like to wow your guests with something remarkably simple but utterly delicious, you really need to try this little gem of an idea I stole from lunching with Will Studd in Margaret River many years ago. Scoop this gooey, garlicky, winey goodness with chunks of torn fresh baguette – if you die tomorrow, all will be well.

FEEDS 2–6

INGREDIENTS

2 garlic cloves, peeled
1 small wheel (about 200 g/7 oz) of the best camembert cheese you can afford, at room temperature
2 tablespoons good-quality red wine
2–3 sprigs of thyme

METHOD

Preheat the oven to 190°C (375°F) fan-forced.

Blanch the garlic in boiling water for about 1 minute. Cool, then quarter each clove lengthways.

If you get a French camembert and it comes in one of those lovely wooden boxes, remove the plastic and leave the cheese in there. If not, fold a rectangular piece of foil about 30 x 15 cm (12 x 6 inches) in half, to make a squarish shape, pop the wheel of cheese on it and scrunch the foil up around the sides to create a little vessel, leaving the top exposed.

Make eight small slits evenly across the surface of the cheese with the tip of a paring knife, and insert the slices of garlic in them. Drizzle the wine over the slits a bit at a time, making sure that the wine is being absorbed. You can pick the thyme or leave as whole sprigs – sprinkle these on top.

Pop the cheese, in its box or foil, on a baking tray, and bake for 10 minutes. You want the middle to be gooey, but the sides to be somewhat intact. Serve immediately, with a baguette or crackers.

Easy Mixed Mushroom & Hazelnut Tarts

In my opinion, there's no better way to eat mushrooms than this. Make sure you caramelise the mushrooms lovingly, so those gorgeous nutty flavours really sing. This mushroom base is brilliant in omelettes and quiches, or over toast.

FEEDS 4–6

INGREDIENTS

6–8 sheets ready-made filo pastry, cut into 13 cm (5 inch) squares
100 g (3½ oz) butter, melted

MIXED MUSHROOMS

600 g (1 lb 5 oz) mixed mushrooms (Swiss browns/cremini, regular buttons, enoki & king oysters are some more common ones)
70 g (2½ oz) butter
Dash of olive oil
12 sprigs of thyme
1 large garlic clove, finely chopped or crushed
90 g (3¼ oz) hazelnuts, roasted & roughly chopped (see first paragraph of Basic Nut Praline method on page 100)
Sea salt & freshly ground black pepper
1 large handful flat-leaf (Italian) parsley, chopped

TO SERVE

375 ml (13 fl oz/1½ cups) crème fraîche
Salt & freshly ground black pepper
3 tablespoons chopped chives

METHOD

Preheat the oven to 200°C (400°F) fan-forced.

To make the tart shells, brush 8–10 layers of the square pieces of filo with butter, and overlap them on one another so that they form a rough circle, then press into the hole of a standard muffin tin. Make four to six of these. Bake for 20 minutes, or until the filo is golden brown. Remove from the oven and set aside.

Meanwhile, combine the mushrooms with half the butter, the olive oil and thyme in a stainless-steel frying pan over medium–high heat, and sauté about 1 minute or until golden. Add the garlic and hazelnuts, and continue cooking the mushrooms until they are nice and brown. Season with salt and pepper, then remove from the heat. Add the parsley, and toss to combine.

To serve, warm the tart shells in a 100°C (200°F) fan-forced oven for about 10 minutes. Remove them from the oven and pile each one high with the mushrooms. Season the crème fraîche with salt and pepper before dolloping on each tart and finishing with a sprinkling of chives.

Mini Pork & Fennel Sausage Rolls

It's wise not to forget about the simple things in life, and a good old-fashioned sauso roll is one of them. I love the mini ones because you get more caramelisation and crunch for your buck and, let's face it, they're a bit naughty, so making them small means you can eat more, right?

MAKES ABOUT 20 MINI SAUSAGE ROLLS

INGREDIENTS

1 quantity Rough Puff Pastry
  (see page 200)
1 egg, lightly whisked, for egg wash

FILLING

2 tablespoons olive oil
3 garlic cloves, crushed
1 small brown onion, finely chopped
2 teaspoons freshly picked thyme
  leaves
2 teaspoons fennel seeds, roughly
  crushed OR chopped
½ teaspoon dried chilli flakes
  OR to taste
500 g (1 lb 2 oz) pork mince
  (ground pork)
1 small pink lady apple, grated
1 heaped tablespoon dried
  breadcrumbs
10 g (¼ oz) salt
1 teaspoon freshly ground black
  pepper

TO SERVE

250 ml (9 fl oz/1 cup) tomato
  ketchup OR tomato sauce

METHOD

To make the filling, heat the olive oil, garlic and onion in a small non-stick frying pan over medium heat, and sauté for about a minute until soft and translucent. Add the thyme, fennel and chilli, and cook for a few seconds until fragrant. Add to the remaining ingredients in a large bowl and, using clean hands, mix thoroughly until well combined. Refrigerate while rolling out the puff pastry.

Preheat the oven to 200°C (400°F) fan-forced. Line two standard baking trays with baking paper.

Roll out your rough puff into a 4 mm (³⁄₁₆ inch) thick, 25 x 60 cm (10 x 24 inch) rectangle. Cut all four edges so you now have a tidy rectangle with straight sides. Next, slice it across the width into four roughly 15 cm (6 inch) strips. Arrange a 4 cm (1½ inch) width of the filling along the length of each strip, making sure you can roll them over to enclose the meat easily. Don't fret if my measurements are not coming to fruition for you. If your pastry is a bit skinny, just place a skinnier strip of filling in it.

To finish, instead of tucking one edge into the roll, leave it open to meet the other edge. Brush some egg wash between the edges and press down with a fork to seal them together. Slice into 4 cm (1½ inch) pieces, then score each parcel with 5 mm (¼ inch) gaps on a diagonal without piercing through the pastry. Place the mini sausage rolls on the prepared trays, and bake for about 30 minutes until a deep golden brown.

Serve hot to have plain or with tomato sauce.

Rosemary Olive Oil Crackers

Once you've made and tasted these, you will never buy crackers again.
They're a cinch to make, incredibly moreish and will keep well for weeks.

MAKES ABOUT 800 G (1 LB 12 OZ) OF CRACKERS

INGREDIENTS

275 g (9¾ oz/1½ cups) semolina
   flour
220 g (7¾ oz/1½ cups) white
   whole-wheat flour OR plain
   (all-purpose) flour + extra,
   for dusting
1 teaspoon salt
250 ml (9 fl oz/1 cup) warm water
80 ml (2½ fl oz/⅓ cup) extra virgin
   olive oil
2–3 tablespoons fresh rosemary,
   finely chopped

METHOD

To make the crackers, combine all the ingredients in the bowl of an electric stand mixer with a dough hook attachment, and hook on the lowest setting for about 2 minutes or until smooth. Knead the dough into a round ball, then place on a lightly floured work surface, covered with a moist tea towel, to rest for 15 minutes.

Preheat the oven to 170°C (325°F) fan-forced.

To roll out the dough, you can do it the old-fashioned way, with a rolling pin, or run it through a pasta maker so you have sheets about 1 mm (¹⁄₁₆ inch) thick. Make sure you keep lightly dusting your work surface and the dough, so it doesn't stick. To cut the crackers, you can use a knife or a rotary cutter used for pizza or making pasta. Cut into whatever shape you want, whether it be dramatic shards that will look stunning on a cheese platter or small squares that are easy to handle.

Bake for about 20 minutes until golden. Cool before storing in an airtight container for 3–4 weeks.

NOTE

If you want to make these by hand, simply follow the same instructions, except use a regular mixing bowl and knead the ingredients until you have a smooth dough.

chapter two
BAKE-SALE BEAUTIES

Orange Yoghurt Hearts with Violet Glaze & Raspberries

The good news is these little picture-perfect cakes use what I call my 'bung-in-and-mix' method. Quite literally, you combine the dry ingredients with the wet ingredients, mix and you're done. The combination of orange, raspberry and violet is sensational. Arranged on a tiered cake stand, these make a charming alternative to a birthday cake.

MAKES 12 MINI CAKES

INGREDIENTS

300 g (10½ oz/2 cups) plain (all-purpose) flour
1 teaspoon bicarbonate of soda (baking soda)
250 g (9 oz) caster (superfine) sugar
½ teaspoon salt
160 g (5¾ oz) unsalted butter, melted
250 g (9 oz/1 cup) Greek-style yoghurt
4 large eggs, lightly whisked
Finely grated zest of 1 orange

VIOLET GLAZE

350 g (12 oz/3 cups) pure icing (confectioners') sugar
3 tablespoons warm water
2 drops pink OR red food colouring
1 or 2 drops violet extract (optional – available online or at specialty shops)

BITS & PIECES

1 punnet fresh raspberries, sliced in half
1 quantity Vanilla Sour Cream (see page 203) OR Yoghurt Mascarpone Cream (see page 206)
Finely grated orange zest (optional)

METHOD

Preheat the oven to 170°C (325°F) fan-forced. Grease and flour a 12-hole mini cake tin well.

Briefly whisk the flour, bicarbonate of soda, sugar and salt in a medium mixing bowl to combine. Add the butter, yoghurt, eggs and zest, then whisk until smooth. Carefully fill the moulds three-quarters of the way, and bake for about 25 minutes until golden brown. As soon as the cakes come out of the oven, tip the tray upside down onto a wire rack, and shake out the cakes. If you leave them too long, the sugars settle and you'll have trouble unmoulding them without leaving bits behind. Allow to cool completely before icing.

To make the glaze, combine the icing sugar mixture, water, food colouring and violet extract in a small bowl, and whisk until smooth. Add more water if you prefer a runnier, translucent consistency like I do. Transfer to a piping bag, and snip a 2 mm (1/16 inch) hole off the tip. Slowly run the glaze in concentric circles working from the centre of each cake outwards, so you can control the drizzle effect running down the sides. Top with a few raspberries.

Serve with your choice of dolloping cream and, if you'd like to bolster the orange flavour, finely grate a smidgen of orange zest over the top. (You can keep any un-iced cakes in an airtight container for up to 5 days.)

Orange Kisses with Cream Cheese Centres

Truly, if a kiss could be embodied in a biscuit, this would be it. These are the shortest shortbreads you will ever encounter, filled with divine salty–sweet orange-infused cream cheese. Instead of lemon juice, I've used white balsamic vinegar, which is sweet and gives a lovely roundness to the acidity. I suggest you fill these as you want to eat them; otherwise they need to be refrigerated and, even though still lovely, won't have that melt-in-your-mouth magic.

MAKES ABOUT 24 SANDWICHED BISCUITS

INGREDIENTS
250 g (9 oz) unsalted butter, softened
½ teaspoon salt
Finely grated zest of ½ orange
60 g (2¼ oz/½ cup) wheaten cornflour (cornstarch), sifted (see note)
225 g (8 oz/1½ cups) plain (all-purpose) flour, sifted

CREAM CHEESE FILLING
250 g (9 oz) cream cheese, at room temperature
50 g (1¾ oz) unsalted butter, softened
Finely grated zest of ½ orange
90 g (3¼ oz/¾ cup) icing (confectioners') sugar
1½ tablespoons white balsamic vinegar

METHOD
Preheat the oven to 170°C (340°F) fan-forced. Line two large baking trays with baking paper.

To make the shortbreads, combine the butter, salt and zest in a medium mixing bowl, and beat with an electric mixer on high speed until pale and fluffy. Add the cornflour and flour, and mix with a wooden spoon until just combined – overmixing will 'unshorten' the mixture. Transfer the mixture to a large piping bag fitted with a 1 cm (½ inch) star nozzle, and pipe 4 cm (1½ inch) rosettes onto the prepared baking trays. You will end up with about 48 biscuit halves. Bake for 15–25 minutes until the kisses are golden brown. Cool completely before filling.

To make the cream cheese filling, combine the cream cheese, butter, zest and half the icing sugar in a medium mixing bowl, and whisk with an electric mixer on high speed until combined. Add the remaining icing sugar, and whisk until pale and fluffy. Add the balsamic vinegar, and whisk by hand until just combined.

Transfer to a piping bag with a 1 cm (½ inch) diameter hole snipped off the tip, and pipe about a teaspoon of filling to sandwich between 2 biscuits. Repeat until all the biscuits are used up. These keep well for up to 2 weeks if kept refrigerated in an airtight container.

NOTE
I only use wheaten cornflour (cornstarch) in my baking. It's not accurately named and it's the old-fashioned stuff everyone used until a few years ago, when gluten intolerances resulted in maize cornstarch becoming more prevalent. Texturally, maize cornflour leaves a grainy residue in the mouth. To be sure what you're getting, always check the ingredients list on the packet.

Madeleines with Strawberry Rosewater Glaze

The brilliant thing about these little French butter cakes is that they age so well but, if you eat them soon after they come out of the oven, you'll catch that small window of crispy edged goodness that can only be experienced if you're an enthusiastic baker – or at least related to one!

MAKES ABOUT 12 MADELEINES

INGREDIENTS

100 g (3½ oz/⅔ cup) plain (all-purpose) flour

1 teaspoon baking powder

120 g (4¼ oz) caster (superfine) sugar

2 eggs, lightly whisked

140 g (5 oz) butter, melted

½ teaspoon finely grated lemon zest

STRAWBERRY ROSEWATER GLAZE

60–90 g (2¼ – 3¼ oz/½–¾ cup) pure icing (confectioners') sugar, sifted

4–6 strawberries, mashed and passed through a sieve

1 teaspoon rosewater

METHOD

In a medium mixing bowl, combine the flour, baking powder and sugar. Mix with a wooden spoon, then add the eggs, butter and lemon zest. Stir until smooth, then transfer the batter to a piping bag, and refrigerate for 2 hours.

Preheat the oven to 200°C (400°F) fan-forced. Grease a 12-hole madeleine tin well.

Pipe a small amount of the batter into each mould, filling them only two-thirds of the way. Reduce the oven temperature to 180°C (350°F) fan-forced, and bake for 10 minutes until the madeleines are golden. As soon as they come out of the oven, smack the edge of the tray onto the work surface to unmould the cakes. If you wait for just a split second too long, you'll find they stick very quickly and you will chuck a tanty like I did the first time I made them because I didn't have this critical bit of information! Allow to cool completely on a wire rack before glazing.

To make the strawberry rosewater glaze, combine the icing sugar, strawberry purée and rosewater in a small bowl, then stir until smooth and quite runny. If it's too thick, mash more strawberries to add to the mixture. Dip just half of each madeleine into the glaze diagonally, then let the glaze set before serving. These keep well for up to a week in an airtight container.

Honey Cardamom Nut Bars

Sugarless, flourless, dairy-less, eggless – yet delicious. Winning.
Oh, and dead easy.

MAKES ABOUT 12 BARS

INGREDIENTS

145 g (5½ oz/1 cup) sunflower seeds
80 g (2¾ oz/scant ½ cup) whole
 natural almonds, roughly
 chopped
70 g (2½ oz/scant ½ cup) pistachio
 nut kernels, roughly chopped
35 g (1¼ oz/½ cup) dried shredded
 coconut
1 teaspoon ground cardamom
½ teaspoon salt
175 g (6 oz/½ cup) honey
Finely grated zest of ½ orange
1 teaspoon rosewater OR orange
 blossom water (optional)

METHOD

Preheat the oven to 180°C (350°F) fan-forced. Line a rectangular baking tin or ovenproof dish about 17 x 21 cm (6½ x 8¼ inches) with baking paper, leaving excess paper on all four sides (so you can lift the entire slab out in one go later).

Combine all the dry ingredients in a medium mixing bowl. Heat the honey in a small saucepan over medium–low heat until warm and runny. Add to the dry ingredients with the zest and rosewater, and fold in with a spoon until all the nuts are coated well with the honey. Tip the mixture into the prepared tin and spread evenly, paying attention to the edges and corners.

Bake for 20 minutes until golden brown, then immediately compress the mixture firmly all over, using a spoon or spatula. Allow to cool completely in the tin, before using the overhanging sides of the baking paper to lift the entire slab out. Cut into bars about 7 x 4 cm (2¾ x 1½ inches).

I like to wrap the centre of each bar with a strip of baking paper and string, so you can pick them up without getting sticky fingers. These make a lovely gift – stored in an airtight container, they will keep well for a couple of weeks.

Kuih Kapit – Coconut Love Letters

These light-as-a-feather Malaysian-style wafers are like an even more delicate version of a tuille, but with a lovely coconut flavour. Traditionally these are made with a cast-iron mould heated over coals, but electric love-letter (kuih kapit) makers are easy to source from online shops. Failing that, a pizelle maker from a specialty homewares shop is your best bet. If you prefer, you can roll the wafers into little tubes instead of folding them into quarters after cooking.

MAKES ABOUT 40 WAFERS

INGREDIENTS
3 large eggs
200 g (7 oz) caster (superfine) sugar
60 g (2¼ oz) plain
    (all-purpose) flour
150 g (5½ oz) rice flour
30 g (1 oz) tapioca flour
250 ml (9 fl oz/1 cup)
    coconut cream
120 ml (4 fl oz/½ cup) water

METHOD
Combine the eggs and sugar in a medium mixing bowl, and whisk well. Add all the flours, and whisk until smooth. Add the coconut cream and water, and whisk until combined.

Preheat the kuih kapit/pizelle maker according to the manufacturer's instructions.

Scoop about 1 tablespoon of batter into each mould, press to sandwich the mixture in place and cook for 1–2 minutes until they are golden. It won't harm the wafer if you are unsure of its colour and need to open the mould during cooking to check. Remove the wafer and quickly fold into quarters, so you have a nice fan shape, then press down on the wafer with a spatula to flatten further. Cool on a wire rack before storing in an airtight container for up to 3 weeks.

Fruitmallows

These are really fun to make and great, natural treats to have around the house. You can use any fruit purée or juice, but punchier flavours such as passionfruit, strawberry, raspberry, mango, banana, apricot or orange will work best. For the orange, I suggest adding the finely grated zest of an orange as well.

MAKES ABOUT 50 FRUITMALLOWS

INGREDIENTS
380 g (13½ oz/1¾ cups) sugar
1 tablespoon liquid glucose
150 ml (5 fl oz) water
140 g (5 oz) egg whites
150 ml (5 fl oz) fruit purée of choice (see introduction above)
20 g (¾ oz) gelatine sheets, soaked in cool water until soft (about 10 minutes)

DREDGING POWDER
50 g (1¾ oz) icing (confectioners') sugar mixture
50 g (1¾ oz) wheaten cornflour (cornstarch), see note on page 33

METHOD
To make the dredging powder, mix the icing sugar and cornflour in a small bowl, then sift a generous layer of it onto two baking trays so that they are well coated. Reserve the remaining dredging powder for later.

Combine the sugar, liquid glucose and water in a small saucepan. Stir with a clean metal spoon and bring to the boil, then leave it alone. Hereon, my method for making this is unorthodox, in that I don't use a thermometer because I don't like them. I go by sight, sound and smell. If you do want to use one, the temperature you want to reach is 118°–125°C (244°–257°F). Otherwise, just boil the sugar until you can see no more steam rising from the mixture. The bubbles will slow down, and the smell of the sugar will become richer.

Meanwhile, whisk the egg whites with an electric stand mixer on high speed until stiff peaks form. Leave the bowl on the stand. Bring the fruit purée to the boil in a small saucepan. After squeezing any excess water away, add the gelatine sheets to the purée and stir until dissolved.

I usually wait until there is the faintest wisp of gold in the sugar before whisking it off the stove. With the electric mixer on high speed already, pour a continuous, very thin thread of sugar into the whisked egg whites until all the mixture has been added, then pour in the fruit–gelatine mixture. Keep whisking until combined, then reduce to the lowest speed to whisk until the bowl feels cool to the touch and the mixture forms stiff peaks.

There are two ways you can finish the fruitmallows: You can pour the mixture onto the prepared tray and spread evenly with a spatula until about 2 cm (¾ inch) thick. Leave to set for 2 hours, then slice into cubes, and toss in the remaining dredging powder to stop the sides from being sticky. Alternatively, pipe dollops of the mixture onto the prepared tray, which looks adorable and I think is more fun to do. Allow to set for 2 hours, then sift more of the dredging powder over the top, to prevent the fruitmallows from sticking to one another. Store in airtight containers for up to 2 weeks.

Wei Yee's Choc Peanut Butter Cupcakes

The first time I tasted these wickedly delicious morsels, made by my friend Wei Yee, I really had to revise my long-standing prejudice against cupcakes. Everything about them is perfection: a featherlight chocolate cake with the most tender crumb, hiding a salty–sweet peanut butter hit under a dollop of crème Chantilly. I could easily inhale half a dozen in a frenzied spell and not realise what just happened.

MAKES 12 CUPCAKES

BATTER

260 g (9¼ oz/1¾ cups) plain (all-purpose) flour, sifted

1½ teaspoons baking powder, sifted

1½ teaspoons bicarbonate of soda (baking soda), sifted

80 g (2¾ oz/¾ cup) Dutch process cocoa powder, sifted

440 g (15½ oz/2 cups) caster (superfine) sugar

1 teaspoon salt

2 eggs

250 ml (9 fl oz/1 cup) milk

125 ml (4 fl oz/½ cup) vegetable oil

2 teaspoons vanilla extract OR vanilla essence

250 ml (9 fl oz/1 cup) boiling water

PEANUT BUTTER FILLING

140 g (5 oz/½ cup) smooth peanut butter

60 g (2¼ oz/½ cup) icing (confectioners') sugar mixture

2 tablespoons thickened (whipping) cream

2 tablespoons milk

TO DECORATE

1 quantity Crème Chantilly, whisked to stiff peaks (see page 203)

METHOD

Preheat the oven to 170°C (325°F) fan-forced. Line a 12-hole standard muffin tin with paper cases.

To make the batter, combine the flour, baking powder, bicarbonate of soda, cocoa, sugar and salt in a medium–large mixing bowl. Add the eggs, milk, vegetable oil and vanilla. Whisk until smooth, then add the boiling water and stir with the whisk until combined. Fill each of the paper cases until two-thirds full. Bake for about 25 minutes, or until an inserted skewer comes out clean. Transfer the cupcakes to a wire rack, and cool completely before filling and decorating.

To make the peanut butter filling, combine the peanut butter and icing sugar in a medium mixing bowl, and whisk with an electric mixer on the highest speed until smooth. Add the cream, and whisk on medium speed very briefly until just combined. Add the milk, and whisk until smooth. Transfer to a piping bag with a 1 cm (½ inch) round nozzle.

To assemble the cupcakes, stick the nozzle into the centre of each cupcake, and pipe about a teaspoon's worth of peanut butter filling into it. Transfer the Crème Chantilly to a piping bag fitted with a 1 cm (½ inch) star nozzle, and pipe rosettes of cream on top of each cupcake. Serve immediately.

Red Velvet Cupcakes

I write this recipe with my tail between my legs because, many moons ago when I didn't understand that red velvet cupcakes were an actual thing, I turned my nose up at the idea of a cake being defined by its colour, rather than its flavour. Then I made it and realised that it's the unique combination of all those things – the lurid colour, the not-quite-discernible chocolate flavour and the all-important vanilla cream cheese frosting – that makes this cupcake legit! You can make this into a single large cake using two round 23 cm (9 inch) tins: sandwich the layers together with the frosting, then ice it completely, so when the finished cake is cut that red velvet pops like nobody's business.

MAKES ABOUT 18 CUPCAKES

BATTER

375 g (13 oz/2½ cups) plain (all-purpose) flour, sifted
2 tablespoons Dutch process cocoa powder, sifted
1 teaspoon bicarbonate of soda (baking soda), sifted
1 teaspoon salt
330 g (11½ oz/1½ cups) caster (superfine) sugar
250 ml (9 fl oz/1 cup) buttermilk
200 g (7 oz) unsalted butter, melted
2 eggs, lightly whisked
1 tablespoon white vinegar
1 teaspoon vanilla extract OR vanilla essence
50 ml (1½ fl oz) red food colouring

CREAM CHEESE FROSTING

375 g (13 oz) cream cheese, at room temperature
100 g (3½ oz) butter, softened
1 teaspoon vanilla bean paste OR vanilla essence
185 g (6 oz/1½ cups) icing (confectioners') sugar

METHOD

Preheat the oven to 170°C (325°F) fan-forced. Line about 18 holes of two 12-hole standard muffin tins with paper cases.

To make the batter, combine the flour, cocoa, bicarbonate of soda, salt and sugar in a large bowl. Whisk briefly to mix the dry ingredients, then add the buttermilk, melted butter, eggs, vinegar, vanilla and food colouring (make sure you use the full amount, or the cake will turn out an underwhelming brown colour), and whisk until smooth. Fill each of the paper cases with the mixture until two-thirds full. Bake for about 20 minutes, or until an inserted skewer comes out clean. Turn out onto a wire rack, and cool completely before icing.

To make the frosting, combine the cream cheese, butter, vanilla and icing sugar in a medium mixing bowl. Using the paddle attachment of an electric mixer, beat together until smooth. Transfer the frosting to a piping bag fitted with a large star nozzle. Pipe a reasonable amount of the frosting on top of each cupcake. These store very well if refrigerated in an airtight container for up to a week, but they are much nicer to eat when brought back to room temperature.

NOTE

If you are ever in a spot trying to find buttermilk, make mock buttermilk instead. Combine 40 ml (1½ fl oz) white vinegar with 210 ml (7½ fl oz) milk to make 250 ml (9 fl oz/1 cup), allow to sit for mere seconds (it will curdle immediately), then use as you would a real buttermilk. The ratio is 1 part vinegar to 5 parts milk.

Priyant's Pecan Double Chocolate Brownies

I'm shocked to have managed to pry this out of my buddy Pri's hands (oh, such terrible puns!) because it *was* a very closely guarded secret. Seriously, it's the *only* recipe I've ever come across that produces the dense, chewy quality that I've chased in a brownie for years. To say Pri is neurotic about getting this perfect is an understatement, seeing as it's in its fourth year of evolution, and I suspect will keep going. I present to you the holy grail of brownies ...

MAKES 24 SQUARES

INGREDIENTS

230 g (8 oz) unsalted butter

230 g (8 oz/1⅔ cups) dark chocolate chips OR chopped dark chocolate

4 eggs, lightly whisked

220 g (8 oz/1 cup) caster (superfine) sugar

220 g (8 oz/1 cup) soft dark brown sugar

2 teaspoons vanilla extract OR vanilla essence

½ teaspoon salt

150 g (5½ oz/1 cup) plain (all-purpose) flour

100 g (3½ oz/⅔ cup) milk chocolate chips OR chopped milk chocolate

75 g (2½ oz/¾ cup) toasted pecans OR walnuts (see first paragraph of Basic Nut Praline method on page 100)

METHOD

Preheat the oven to 160°C (315°F) fan-forced. Line a rectangular baking tin or ovenproof dish, roughly 33 x 24 x 4 cm (9½ x 13 x 1½ inches), with a single sheet of baking paper that overhangs the sides.

Melt the butter in a large heatproof bowl in the microwave or in a medium saucepan over medium heat. Add the dark chocolate, and whisk until smooth. If using a saucepan, remove from the heat before adding the chocolate.

In a medium mixing bowl, whisk the eggs, two sugars, vanilla and salt until combined. Add the butter and chocolate mixture, and whisk until combined. Add the flour, and whisk until smooth. Fold in the milk chocolate and pecans, then pour the batter into the prepared tin or dish.

Bake for 45 minutes, or until an inserted skewer comes out clean. Chill before cutting. (Refrigerating overnight will give the brownies a particularly lovely chewy texture.) Store in the refrigerator in an airtight container, and the brownies will keep well for up to 2 weeks.

Sarah's Raspberry Financiers

These are amongst my favourite things that Sarah makes. It is said that these little cakes became popular in the financial district of Paris because of their resemblance to the shape of a gold bar and the ease with which they could be stored in pockets. Another story suggests they were the invention of an order of nuns from the Middle Ages. The thing that distinguishes their flavour is the subtle nuttiness of the browned butter embedded in a dense chewy cake, which, by the way, just keeps and keeps ... if self-control is your 'thing'.

MAKES 12 FINANCIERS

INGREDIENTS

80 g (2¾ oz) unsalted butter

150 g (5½ oz/1¼ cups) icing (confectioners') sugar

50 g (1¾ oz/½ cup) almond meal

60 g (2¼ oz) plain (all-purpose) flour

½ teaspoon baking powder

5 egg whites

½ teaspoon almond extract

90 g (3½ oz/¾ cup) fresh or frozen raspberries

25 g (1 oz/¼ cup) flaked almonds

METHOD

Preheat the oven to 170°C (325°F) fan-forced. Line 12 financier moulds with baking paper.

Melt the butter in a small frying pan over medium heat, and cook until foamy and dotted with brown flecks. Set aside.

In a medium mixing bowl, briefly whisk the icing sugar, almond meal, flour and baking powder to combine. Add the egg whites, almond extract and browned butter, and whisk until smooth.

Fill each prepared mould three-quarters to the top with the mixture, then dot each one with 3 or 4 raspberries. Sprinkle each with a few flaked almonds, and bake for 10–15 minutes, or until golden brown and an inserted skewer comes out clean. Using the paper lining, lift the financiers out of the moulds and onto a wire rack. Cool completely before storing in an airtight container. In a good old-fashioned biscuit tin, these keep for up to 2 weeks, but keep refrigerated during summer.

Malaysian Pineapple Tarts

Pineapple tarts are a Malaysian cottage-industry classic. I prefer a biscuity base rather than a rich traditional short pastry, so I use my faithful almond pâte sablée instead. Do make sure to stash some away for yourself or your family and friends will converge on them like vultures and inhale them like there's no tomorrow. If you are an impatient cook, I advise you skip the embellishing. Just get that jam on the pastry, bake and scoot those into your tummy ASAP. Also, if you want to get all proper Malaysian, you can easily buy pineapple tart moulds/cutters like the one I've used from specialty online shops.

MAKES ABOUT 30 TARTS

INGREDIENTS
Plain (all-purpose) flour,
　for dusting
1 quantity Almond Pâte Sablée
　(see page 209)
1 egg, whisked, for egg wash

PINEAPPLE JAM
750 ml (26 fl oz/3 cups) pineapple
　purée
330 g (11½ oz/1½ cups) sugar

METHOD
To make the pineapple purée, cut 750 g (1 lb 10 oz) of fresh pineapple into rough chunks and blitz until you have a rough purée. You can use tinned pineapple rings instead. If using tinned, drain before blitzing and reduce the amount of sugar for the jam to 220 g (7¾ oz/1 cup).

Combine the pineapple purée and sugar in a medium non-stick saucepan. Stir and bring to the boil. Reduce to a simmer and stir every few minutes, until the jam reduces to a thick paste with no remaining liquid. As the mixture thickens, you will have to stir more frequently. Spread out on a dinner plate to cool, then with wet hands roll into balls the size of small marbles. Set aside.

Preheat the oven to 180°C (350°F) fan-forced.

To cut out the tart bases, lightly flour your work surface. Roll out the pastry until 5–7 mm (about ¼ inch) thick, then cut the bases using a 4 cm (1½ inch) round pastry cutter. Cut out all the bases at once, to streamline your tasks.

Next, press the back of a melon baller into the centre of each tart base, to make a half-sphere indentation. If you want to decorate each tart more, use the blunt end of a skewer to stab a ring of small dimples around the edge of each base. Brush with the egg wash, including around the sides, then pop a ball of the pineapple jam into the indentation and press to flatten the surface slightly.

Bake for about 20 minutes until the pastry is golden. Cool completely on a wire rack, before storing in an airtight container. These will easily keep for up to 3 weeks.

Rhino & Tim's Chicken Liver Treats

First, let's be clear, these biscuits are for dogs, not humans!
If you're like me and get a bit stressy about the dodgy regulations
that surround pet food, you can make your own. My guys, Rhino
and Tim, are totally obsessed with these, and the best thing is
that they're incredibly easy to whip up.

MAKES ABOUT 1 KG (2 LB 4 OZ) DOG BISCUITS

INGREDIENTS

600 g (1 lb 5 oz/4 cups) wholemeal
    (whole-wheat) flour + extra, for
    sprinkling
165 g (5¾ oz/1½ cups)
    powdered milk
75 g (2½ oz/1 cup) wheat germ
½ teaspoon garlic powder
500 g (1 lb 2 oz) chicken livers
3 eggs
30 g (1 oz/1 cup) roughly chopped
    flat-leaf (Italian) parsley,
    including stalks

METHOD

Preheat the oven to 110°C (225°F) fan-forced.

Combine all the dry ingredients in a food processor, and pulse very briefly to mix. Add the livers, eggs and parsley, then pulse until the mixture gathers into a rough dough.

Turn out onto a floured work surface, sprinkle more wholemeal flour on top and roll until 6 mm (¼ inch) thick. Slice roughly into 4 cm (1½ inch) squares, and bake for 1–1½ hours until dry and crunchy. If the bikkies seem a little rubbery when you take them out of the oven, don't be concerned – they'll turn super-crunchy on cooling.

Cool completely before storing in an airtight container, then use freely to manipulate your fur children into good behaviour! These keep well in an airtight container for up to 2 months.

NOTE

Just so you know, these dog biscuits are designed to be used as treats, not a kibble substitute.

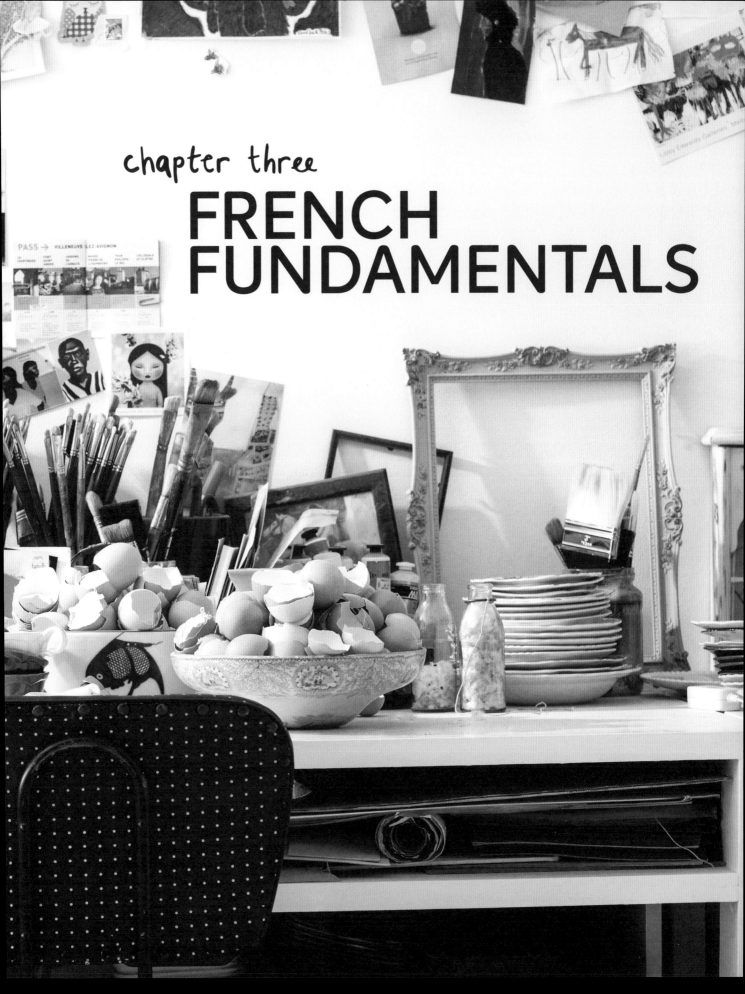

chapter three
FRENCH FUNDAMENTALS

Classic Brioche

Put simply, brioche is a lovely cakey bread that you can use in a savoury or sweet context. Slice up and toast to have with mushrooms cooked in butter, thyme and garlic, or soak in a vanilla custard mixture to pan-fry into a heavenly French toast that's so soft you can scoop it with a spoon. This is an excellent beginners' bread to make because its technical requirements are low.

MAKES 2 X 20 CM (8 INCH) LOAVES

INGREDIENTS

600 g (1 lb 5 oz/4 cups) plain (all-purpose) flour + extra, for dusting
2 teaspoons dried yeast
120 ml (4 fl oz/½ cup) tepid milk
3 tablespoons caster (superfine) sugar
150 g (5½ oz) unsalted butter, softened
6 eggs
15 g (½ oz) fine salt

EGG WASH

1 egg, whisked well

METHOD

Combine the flour, yeast, milk, sugar, butter and eggs in the bowl of an electric stand mixer with a dough hook attachment. Hook on the lowest setting for 5 minutes until you have a sticky, shiny, very wet dough – it will be almost paste-like. Add the salt, and mix for a further 1–2 minutes, then cover well with plastic wrap and refrigerate the dough overnight.

The next day, preheat the oven to 190°C (375°F) fan-forced. Line two standard loaf tins (about 22 x 10 x 6 cm/8½ x 4 x 2½ inches) with baking paper.

Scrape the dough onto a well-floured work surface. Divide into two even portions, and knead each one very briefly. Roll each piece of dough into a smooth, fat sausage that fits into each of the prepared tins. Allow to rise in a draught-free spot in the house – and a warm one if possible – until doubled in size. To test whether the dough has 'proven', or risen, sufficiently, just shake the tins of brioche slightly, and they should wobble voluptuously.

Baste with the egg wash, then bake for 10 minutes. Reduce the oven temperature to 180°C (350°F) fan-forced, and bake for another 30 minutes. The brioche should emerge the most fabulous deep golden brown. To test, insert a skewer to see whether it comes out clean, or do the knock test on the bottom of the loaf – it should sound hollow and similar to the sound that resonates through your head when you knock on your skull, as opposed to a dull thud. Turn the loaves out of the tins, and allow to cool on a wire rack.

This brioche freezes very well, but make sure you cool the loaves completely first.

Perfect Brioche Buns

It's impossible not to glow with pride and feel like a merry little homemaker when you make these. To see these emerge from the oven bathed in the most glorious glossy golden brown is the most deeply satisfying thing. Soft, springy and mildly sweet, they're perfect little things to stuff with pulled meats or use as a lovely dinner roll.

MAKES 8 BUNS

INGREDIENTS
250 ml (9 fl oz/1 cup) warm water
3 tablespoons warm milk
2 teaspoons dried yeast
2½ tablespoons caster
    (superfine) sugar
450 g (1 lb/3 cups) plain
    (all-purpose) flour, sifted
    + extra, for dusting
50 g (1¾ oz/⅓ cup) tipo 00
    strong flour, sifted
40 g (1½ oz) unsalted butter,
    softened
1 large egg, whisked
1¼ teaspoons salt

EGG WASH
1 large egg, whisked with
    1 teaspoon milk

METHOD
Combine the warm water, milk, yeast and sugar in a bowl. Stir until the sugar has dissolved, cover with a plate and let it stand for 5 minutes, or until there are bubbles on the surface of the liquid.

Briefly use a whisk to mix together the two flours in the bowl of an electric stand mixer. Rub the butter into the flour until you have a crumbly mixture. Place the bowl on the stand with the dough hook attachment, add the egg and yeast mixture, and hook on the lowest setting for 2 minutes. Add the salt, and hook for a further 8 minutes until the dough becomes sticky and elastic. Scrape onto a well-floured work surface, pull the sides of the dough into the centre, then pop it seam side down in a lightly greased bowl. Cover with plastic wrap, and refrigerate overnight.

Divide the dough into eight equal portions. Cradle a portion in one hand, while pulling the edges and tucking onto the centre with the other hand until you have a nice round shape. Turn the ball of dough over so that the seam is underneath, then cup the top of the dough, pressing it ever so gently into the work surface, and roll in a circular motion to shape it further into a ball. Repeat until you have 8 balls.

Place each ball about 5 cm (2 inches) apart on a baking tray lined with baking paper. Cover loosely with a clean tea towel, and allow to rise in a draught-free spot – and a warm one if possible – in the house for 1 hour, or until the buns have expanded by another half of their original volume. To check whether they are ready, shake the tray and they should wobble lusciously.

Preheat the oven to 190°C (375°F) fan-forced.

Brush each bun thoroughly with the egg wash, and bake for 15–20 minutes until golden brown. Cool on a wire rack before using. These refrigerate very well in an airtight container or zip-lock plastic bag for up to 2 weeks.

Croissants

I'm not going to lie. The croissant-making 'journey' is laced with equal parts deep satisfaction and hair-tearing frustration. In short, if you choose to enter the croissant vortex, it's a commitment/long-term project to get it right and, when you do, you can *know* at the end that you have become an excellent baker. One major thing to take note of is that the flour-and-water dough and the butter should be the same consistency. If the butter is harder than the dough, it will shatter into large clumps during the laminating process – that is layering butter into dough. As a result, the pastry will not be able to take hold of these uneven clumps, and you'll find the layers not separating well, with a lot of the fat rendering out during baking. If you swap the issues, butter softer than the dough will wind up oozing all over the shop and too thin, so the layers don't puff apart when baked. PS Love handles may be gained during the weeks leading up to harnessing this mad skill.

MAKES 11–13 CROISSANTS

YEAST DOUGH

500 g (1 lb 2 oz/3⅓ cups) strong white flour (no less than 18% protein/gluten is best) + extra, for dusting

3 teaspoons dried yeast

55 g (2 oz/¼ cup) caster (superfine) sugar

140 ml (4½ fl oz) milk

140 ml (4½ fl oz) water

25 g (1 oz) butter, melted

1½ teaspoons salt

250 g (9 oz) chilled unsalted butter

METHOD

To make the yeast dough, combine the flour, yeast, sugar, milk, water and melted butter in the bowl of an electric stand mixer with a dough hook attachment. Hook on the lowest speed for 1 minute. Add the salt, and hook for another 2 minutes. The dough should be beautifully smooth and not be sticking to the side of the bowl, nor to your work surface when you give the dough a brief knead. Shape it into a disc, then pop it on a plate lined with baking paper. Cover in plastic wrap, and rest overnight in the refrigerator.

To laminate your dough, take the 250 g (9 oz) unsalted butter out of the refrigerator, and slice into nine even slices. Join them up on a piece of baking paper, so they form a square. Place another piece of baking paper on top and rest for 15 minutes, then beat lightly with a rolling pin to flatten the butter into a single 20 cm (8 inch) square.

Take the flour-and-water dough out of the refrigerator. Roll and pat into a 26 cm (10½ inch) square, then place the butter at the centre so that it sits like a diamond within the square. Pull the sides to the centre like an envelope, and roll into a rectangle three times as long as it is wide. Fold into thirds, turn 90 degrees clockwise and repeat the process. This is called a 'turn'. Do one more turn (three turns in total), then cover with plastic wrap and refrigerate for 1 hour, or overnight if you want.

To cut the croissants, remove plastic wrap and place the dough on a lightly floured work surface. Roll out the dough into a 60–70 x 20 cm (24–27½ x 8 inch) rectangle about 5 mm (¼ inch) thick. Using a pressing down not dragging action, sparingly slice the uneven edges away, so you have a long rectangle with clean sides. With a clean ruler, mark out 10 cm (4 inch) intervals along the length of the dough. Using a large knife or pizza cutter, again using a pressing not dragging action, cut long triangles with the top point lining up with the centre (5 cm/ 2 inch mark) of each triangle base. Cut a vertical 2 cm (¾ inch) notch at the centre of each of the bases, then gently part these small corners and begin to roll each triangle forward, using the tip as a guide to keep the croissant shape symmetrical. Roll snugly but gently so you don't ruin the lamination. Sit the croissants so their tips are tucked underneath, and space them about 5 cm (2 inches) apart on a baking tray lined with baking paper.

When the tray is filled, place another piece of baking paper on top, then loosely cover with plastic wrap. Rest, or 'prove', in a warm place for about 1 hour until the croissants have doubled in volume. They should wobble if you shake the tray, and feel very light and spongy, springing back easily when gently prodded. If it's a cold day this can take several hours, so patience is key here. Don't rush and bake them if they haven't expanded properly, or you'll get a tiny, heavy nugget of a croissant that's not very nice to eat and, even sadder, you'll be left feeling really discouraged. This is the part where I've gone wrong the most!

Preheat the oven to 200°C (400°F) fan-forced. Remove the plastic wrap and baking paper from the top of the croissants and bake for 10 minutes. Reduce the oven temperature to 180°C (350°F) fan-forced, and bake for another 20 minutes until the croissants are a deep golden brown. Transfer the croissants to a wire rack and, when cooled completely, store in an airtight cake tin for up to a week. Reheat in a 160°C (315°F) fan-forced oven for 10–15 minutes when you want to refresh them. Good luck!

CRACKLE CHOUX BUNS
WITH PISTACHIO
CUSTARD

Crackle Choux Buns with Pistachio Custard

In Paris, there are pâtisseries dedicated entirely to the choux bun, or profiterole, and they always look like this, with a crackle surface, which gives the bun a delicate crunch. They are filled with every possible flavour of custard that you can imagine. Don't listen to anyone who says these are difficult to make. Just follow the recipe carefully, and you'll be fine!

MAKES ABOUT 20 BUNS

PISTACHIO PRALINE

60 g (2¼ oz) pistachio nut kernels, toasted (see first paragraph of Basic Nut Praline method on page 100)
50 g (1¾ oz) caster (superfine) sugar
1 tablespoon water

PISTACHIO CUSTARD

½ quantity chilled Crème Pâtissière (see page 204)
A few drops of green food colouring
150 ml (5 fl oz) thickened (whipping) cream, whisked to stiff peaks

CRACQUELIN

45 g (1½ oz/scant ¼ cup) plain (all-purpose) flour
45g (1½ oz/¼ cup lightly packed) soft brown sugar
35 g (1¼ oz) unsalted butter, softened

CHOUX PASTRY

75 g (2½ oz) butter
185 ml (6 fl oz/¾ cup) water
⅛ teaspoon salt
110 g (3¾ oz/¾ cup) plain (all-purpose) flour
3 eggs

METHOD

To begin, make the pistachio praline. Spread the toasted pistachios on a baking tray lined with baking paper. Combine the sugar and water in a small, heavy-based saucepan. Stir to combine, then leave it alone. Bring to the boil and then watch very carefully from the moment it turns golden. When it turns to a deep amber colour, immediately remove from the heat and pour over the nuts on the baking tray. When the praline has set and cooled, break chunks of it into a mortar. Use the pestle to pound the chunks until you have a fine powder. If you work the mixture a lot, the oils from the nuts might turn the powder into a paste, which is fine.

To make the pistachio custard filling, follow the instructions for Crème Pâtissière on page 204, then fold in the food colouring and the powdered pistachio praline. Chill the custard completely, before whisking in the cream.

To make the craquelin, combine the flour, brown sugar and butter in a small bowl, and mash with a rubber spatula until mixed into a thick paste. Roll between two pieces of baking paper until 1–2 mm (about ⅙ inch) thick. Chill until needed.

Preheat the oven to 200°C (400°F) fan-forced.

Combine the butter, water and salt in a medium non-stick saucepan over medium heat, and wait until the butter has just melted – you don't want the mixture to boil. Add the flour, and keep cooking, stirring continuously with a wooden spoon, until the mixture leaves the side of the saucepan and gathers into a ball. Add the eggs, one at a time, beating until smooth before adding the next.

Transfer the mixture to a piping bag fitted with a 1 cm (½ inch) round nozzle, and pipe 3–4 cm (1¼–1½ inch) dollops with a 3 cm (1¼ inch) gap between them. Take the craquelin out of the refrigerator and, using a pastry cutter, cut enough 4 cm (1½ inch) circles to cover each choux bun. Gently peel them from the baking paper, and pop one on top of each bun. If the circles start to wilt, pop the sheet of cracquelin into the freezer for 2 minutes before continuing.

Bake for 20 minutes until golden brown. As soon as the choux buns come out of the oven, pierce the bottoms with the tip of a piping nozzle to release the steam, and cool them on a wire rack.

To fill the choux buns, pipe the pistachio custard into the holes in the bottom of each bun until you can feel they are filled enough. I find slightly underfilling with the custard makes for a better eating experience. Too much custard can be difficult to eat and too rich on the palate. Serve immediately.

Coffee Éclairs

As a survivor of the 2009 first-ever Zumbo croquembouche challenge on *MasterChef Australia*, I did suffer some post-choux trauma. Only last year did I endeavour to overcome my choux phobia. Funnily enough, it turns out that making 16 slightly crooked éclairs in your own time is a cinch when compared to 100 profiteroles that you then have to turn into a tower of amazingness using digits that have been incinerated by molten sugar within a horribly misconceived time frame. PS These are really yummy.

MAKES ABOUT 16 ÉCLAIRS

CHOUX PASTRY
75 g (2½ oz) butter
185 ml (6 fl oz/¾ cup) water
⅛ teaspoon salt
110 g (3¾ oz/¾ cup) plain
    (all-purpose) flour
3 eggs

COFFEE GLAZE
1–2 tablespoons instant coffee
    granules
2 tablespoons hot water
125–185 g (4½–6½ oz/1–1½ cups)
    icing (confectioners') sugar, sifted

BITS & PIECES
1½ quantities Crème Chantilly,
    whisked to medium peaks
    (see page 203)
40 g (1½ oz) dark chocolate melts
    (buttons) OR chopped dark
    chocolate

METHOD
Preheat the oven to 220°C (425°F) fan-forced.

Combine the butter, water and salt in a medium non-stick saucepan over medium heat, and wait until the butter has just melted – you don't want the mixture to boil. Add the flour, and keep cooking, stirring continuously with a wooden spoon, until the mixture leaves the side of the saucepan and gathers into a ball. Add the eggs, one at a time, beating until smooth before adding the next.

Using a piping bag fitted with a 1 cm (½ inch) round nozzle, pipe straight 12 cm (4½ inch) lines of the choux pastry onto a baking tray lined with baking paper, leaving a 4 cm (1½ inch) space between each éclair (you will end up with about 16 éclairs).

Bake for 30 minutes until the éclairs are puffed and golden. To let the steam out, immediately slice each éclair partially lengthways, leaving half attached for ease of handling later. Cool completely before assembling.

Transfer the Crème Chantilly to a piping bag fitted with a 1 cm (½ inch) nozzle. Open an éclair and pipe along the length of one half, then close to sandwich together. Repeat until all éclairs are filled.

To make the coffee glaze, dissolve the coffee in the hot water, then whisk in the icing sugar until smooth and thick. Dip the top of each éclair into the icing, wiping away any excess with your finger.

Melt the chocolate in a small heatproof bowl in 30-second bursts in the microwave or over a double boiler. Stir until smooth, then transfer to a piping bag. Line up the filled éclairs alongside one another, then snip a tiny 1 mm (¹⁄₂₄ inch) hole off the tip of the piping bag. Run a thin zigzag of chocolate over the glaze. Serve immediately.

Prune & Armagnac Breton

When I roll out the pastry for this hundred-year-old recipe, I imagine hands a century ago going through the same motions, and I feel something magical that defies time and place. Thank goodness for the true caretakers of tradition, passionate artisans such as my French pastry chef friend Eric Pernoud, who are not secretive with their knowledge. What a privilege it is to inherit such a precious thing and allow it to be the time traveller it should be. Now it is yours ... *Bisous* to you for sharing, Eric!

FEEDS 12

PRUNE PURÉE
500 g (1 lb 2 oz/2½ cups) pitted prunes
Enough freshly squeezed orange juice to just cover the prunes
30 ml (1 fl oz) Armagnac OR best-quality brandy you can afford

BRETON PASTRY
250 g (9 oz) unsalted butter, softened
220 g (7¾ oz/1 cup) caster (superfine) sugar
½ teaspoon salt
1 tablespoon rum
5 egg yolks
450 g (1 lb/3 cups) plain (all-purpose) flour + extra, for dusting

EGG WASH
1 egg, whisked

METHOD
To make the prune purée, combine the prunes and orange juice in a medium non-stick saucepan over medium heat. Simmer until the prunes are soft enough to be whisked into a rough purée. Remove from the heat, add the Armagnac and whisk to combine. Cool to room temperature, then transfer to a piping bag.

To make the Breton pastry, beat the butter, sugar and salt with an electric mixer until pale and fluffy. Add the rum and then the egg yolks, one at a time, beating well between each addition. Stir in the flour with a wooden spoon.

Divide the pastry in half, and shape into two discs. Lightly flour the discs and roll out each one directly onto baking paper into an 8 mm (⅜ inch) thick circle. Next, use anything circular with a 25 cm (10 inch) diameter to trace and cut around, so you end up with two same-sized discs. Cover each disc with plastic wrap, and rest in the refrigerator for 15 minutes.

Preheat the oven to 170°C (325°F) fan-forced.

Unwrap the pastry. Slide one disc of pastry (already on the baking paper), onto a baking tray. Snip about 1.5 cm (⅝ inch) off the tip of the piping bag and, starting 2 cm (¾ inch) in from the edge, pipe the prune purée in concentric circles, working from the outside in. Brush the egg wash around the bare border, then lay the second disc of pastry carefully over the top. Now brush the top very generously with the egg wash, taking care that you don't miss any bits. Use a paring knife to lightly drag a lattice pattern through the egg wash.

Bake for about 30 minutes until the top is beautifully golden. This Breton keeps well for about a week and is in fact nicer after a few days, when the pastry has softened.

Palmiers

When one of these heart-shaped beauties shatters between your lips, it's hard to deny the genius of French technique. I mean, with a few meagre ingredients, you have the ability to create this wonderfully delicious thing. They're easy to make but, if you're like me and love the pleasant bitterness that comes from your sugar being cooked right to the edge of being burnt, you kinda need to park yourself in front of the oven in those final moments of cooking to get it just right. If the idea of making the pastry from scratch completely wigs you out, just grab some ready-made butter puff from the shops.

MAKES 12–14 PALMIERS

INGREDIENTS

1 quantity Rough Puff Pastry
   (see page 200)
330 g (11½ oz/1½ cups) caster
   (superfine) sugar

METHOD

To roll out the pastry dough, use the caster sugar instead of 'flouring' your work surface. Sprinkle a good amount on top of the pastry dough as well, before rolling it out until it is about 5 mm (¼ inch) thick and forms a rectangle about 25 x 50 cm (10 x 20 inches). Don't worry if you are a few centimetres off here or there, providing the thickness is still correct.

Trim the shorter ends, so you have straight edges. Now imagine a centre line cutting across the shorter length of the pastry. Fold or roll each side three times, sprinkling each layer with sugar, until they meet at the centre line, then proceed with the fourth roll, which will join the two sides together. At this point you should have a flattish sausage with its cross-section looking like two scrolls meeting in the centre, to make an apple-like shape. Carefully cover with plastic wrap, and freeze for 15–20 minutes.

Meanwhile, preheat the oven to 230°C (450°F) fan-forced.

Line a large baking tray with baking paper, and sprinkle 1 teaspoon caster sugar at 10 cm (4 inch) intervals. Remove the plastic wrap from the palmier scroll, cut into slices 1 cm (½ inch) thick and place them on the patches of sugar on the baking tray. Shimmy them around so the sugar sits flat against the palmier. Sprinkle a little more sugar on top of each one. Bake right away for about 12 minutes until the sugar is beautifully caramelised, keeping in mind that a few burnt edges are a good thing. Otherwise the palmiers will taste too sweet.

When the palmiers come out of the oven, flip them over right away on the baking paper, so you don't get a pool of sugar sticking to them – this is the good side. Be very careful because the sugar will be molten hot. Cool completely, before storing in an airtight container for up to 3 days.

Grand Marnier Chocolate Soufflé

Soufflés are definitely THAT dish that puts the fear of failure in everyone. All you need to know is … grease the ramekins correctly and don't overbeat the egg whites. If you adhere to both these things religiously, you are 60 per cent of the way to making successful soufflés.

MAKES 6 POTS

GREASING

20 g (¾ oz) unsalted butter, softened
2–3 scant tablespoons caster (superfine) sugar

SOUFFLÉ BATTER

180 ml (6 fl oz/¾ cup) milk
100 g (3½ oz) caster (superfine) sugar
1 egg + 1 extra yolk
2 tablespoons plain (all-purpose) flour
½ teaspoon wheaten cornflour (cornstarch), see note on page 33
120 g (4¼ oz) good-quality dark chocolate (70% cocoa solids), chopped, OR dark chocolate melts (buttons)
60 ml (2 fl oz/¼ cup) Grand Marnier OR Frangelico liqueur
6 egg whites
Large pinch of salt

TO SERVE

1 quantity unwhisked (pouring consistency) Crème Chantilly (see page 203)

METHOD

Brush six 200 ml (7 fl oz) capacity straight-sided ramekins with the softened butter. Coat the bottoms well, then on the sides, use only an upward motion so the brush strokes are vertical. This will encourage the soufflé to rise evenly. Coat all greased ramekins with sugar, taking care not to miss any spots. Turn each ramekin upside down on your work surface, and tap to release any excess sugar. Set aside.

To make the soufflé batter, microwave the milk in a heatproof bowl for 1½ minutes on the highest setting. Meanwhile, combine only 80 g (2¾ oz) of the caster sugar and the whole egg and extra yolk in a large bowl, and whisk until pale and thick. Add the flour and cornflour, and whisk until smooth. Pour in the hot milk, and whisk until combined. Keep blitzing in the microwave for 1-minute bursts, whisking well in between. When the batter becomes very thick, add the chocolate and whisk until melted and smooth. Add the Grand Marnier (if using), and whisk until combined. Set aside.

Preheat the oven to 190°C (375°F) fan-forced.

This next part is where you need to pay attention. Using an electric mixer, whisk the egg whites with the salt and remaining 20 g (¾ oz) sugar in a medium mixing bowl until *soft* peaks form. Add one-quarter of the mixture to the chocolate batter, and whisk to loosen the mixture. Add the remaining egg whites and using the whisk, fold the egg whites in as gently as possible until combined.

Fill the prepared ramekins right to the top with the batter, then, using the back of a knife, scrape away any excess mixture to create a perfectly flat surface on each one. Wipe around the edges and sides, and place all the ramekins on a baking tray to bake for 17 minutes for a custardy, molten centre or 19 minutes for a set, more spongy texture.

Serve immediately with the unwhisked Crème Chantilly.

Rhubarb & Spiced Orange Brûlée

This combo just works so well – the tartness of the rhubarb with the richly spiced custard under a faintly bitter crust of caramelised sugar. If the infusion is too much for you to manage, you can omit the spices and just go for the orange zest or plain vanilla-flavoured custard.

FEEDS 6

RHUBARB COMPOTE
250 g (9 oz) rhubarb stalks, sliced into 2 cm (¾ inch) pieces (about 2 cups)
60 g (2¼ oz) caster (superfine) sugar
60 ml (2 fl oz/¼ cup) water

ORANGE CUSTARD
200 ml (7 fl oz) milk
300 ml (10½ fl oz) thin (pouring) cream
1 teaspoon finely grated orange zest
1 cinnamon stick, roughly crushed
2 green cardamom pods, bashed
1.5 cm (⅝ inch) piece of ginger, bashed
5 egg yolks
75 g (2½ oz/⅓ cup) caster (superfine) sugar
1 teaspoon vanilla bean paste OR vanilla extract

TO FINISH
3 tablespoons raw (demerara) sugar (see tip)

METHOD
Preheat the oven to 100°C (200°F) fan-forced.

To make the compote, combine the rhubarb, sugar and water in a small saucepan, and bring to the boil. Reduce the heat and simmer, covered, for about 10 minutes until softened, then whisk to break up the threads. Divide the rhubarb among six 9–10 cm (3½–4 inch) ramekins with 5 cm (2 inch) sides, and spread the mixture to cover the bottom of each dish.

To make the custard, microwave the milk, cream, orange zest, cinnamon, cardamom and ginger in a heatproof bowl for 3 minutes on the highest setting. Cool, then cover and refrigerate for 2 hours. Meanwhile, in a medium mixing bowl, whisk together the yolks and sugar until pale and thick. Using a sieve, strain the infused milk into the yolk-and-sugar mixture. Add the vanilla, then microwave for 2-minute bursts on the highest setting until it is thickened and easily coats the back of a wooden spoon. If the mixture splits a little, bung it all into a blender and blitz on high speed to see if it can be salvaged.

Divide the custard evenly among the ramekins, place them on a baking tray and bake for 20–30 minutes until just set – the custard should be wobbly still. Allow to cool, before transferring to the refrigerator to chill completely.

When ready to serve, sprinkle a teaspoon of the raw sugar on the surface of each brûlée, and torch until the sugar caramelises and forms a crust. It's good to have a few quite dark spots, as this will add a lovely bitterness. If you don't have a blowtorch, simply place very close to the preheated element of a hot grill (broiler), and watch carefully.

TIP
The larger the grains of sugar, the easier they will caramelise because of the cavities surrounding the granules, which allow the heat to circulate. Fine sugar is too dense for the heat to penetrate and will more than likely burn black on melting.

RHUBARB & SPICED
ORANGE BRÛLÉE

MILLY-FILLY AKA MILLE-FEUILLE AKA
FRENCH VANILLA SLICE

Milly-Filly aka Mille-Feuille aka French Vanilla Slice

These really-difficult-to-eat proper vanilla slices rocked my world when I first visited Paris. Paper-thin layers of buttery pastry baked until just before burnt, then layered with dreamy vanilla custard. Puh-leeease hear me out when I say to bake the puff until it is the deepest golden brown because this gorgeous caramelisation I speak of is where the flavour's at. If you don't, you will get an insipid blonde bit of pastry that has not reached its most delicious potential, and a small culinary tragedy will have taken place.

MAKES ABOUT 8 VERY DECENT-SIZED SLICES

INGREDIENTS
1 quantity Rough Puff Pastry
   (see page 200)
1 quantity chilled Crème Pâtissière
   (see page 204)
1 quantity Crème Chantilly,
   whisked to stiff peaks
   (see page 203)

METHOD
To bake the puff, preheat the oven to 190°C (375°F) fan-forced. You will need four to six identical baking trays, which can stack snugly on top of each other, all lined with baking paper. Roll out the puff pastry into 4 mm (³⁄₁₆ inch) thick rectangles – the exact dimensions will be determined by the size of your baking trays, so roll them as large as you can to avoid shrinkage. Place a pastry rectangle onto a lined tray, and lay another sheet of baking paper on top of the puff. Weigh down with a same-sized tray, then, on top of that, another heavy ovenproof object to prevent the puff from rising too much. Repeat until you have used up the pastry.

Bake for about 12 minutes, then reduce the oven temperature to 180°C (350°F) fan-forced, and bake for another 20 minutes until the pastry is a deep golden brown. Do check it every 7 minutes if you are unsure, as all domestic ovens will vary significantly. When the puff comes out of the oven, use oven mitts to press down gently on the top tray to compress any parts that have puffed unevenly, then leave to cool completely on the tray.

To cut, use the baking paper to drag each cooled puff off its tray, onto your work surface. Using a large sharp knife, cut the puff using a sliding, not pressing, action, to avoid shattering the delicate layers of pastry. First, trim the sides so the edges are as straight as possible. Next, divide your cooked puff into uniform rectangles. Bear in mind you want no wastage and that each Milly-Filly has three layers of puff. Mine are usually about 4 x 8 cm (1½ x 3¼ inches). Don't turf the pastry trimmings! Keep them to sprinkle over ice cream or custard – very yum.

Just before using, whisk the Crème Pâtissière briefly, to loosen and smooth out the custard. Transfer to a piping bag, and snip a 7 mm (⅜ inch) hole off the tip.

To assemble your Milly-Filly, pipe two dots of custard onto the serving plate to stop it sliding around. Lay the first piece of puff on top, and pipe the Crème Pâtissière in even pairs of blobs down the length of the pastry. Place another piece of puff on top, press down gently onto the custard to secure, then repeat.

To finish, transfer the Crème Chantilly to a piping bag with a 7 mm (⅜ inch) hole snipped off the tip. Pipe a squiggle of Crème Chantilly to cover the final piece of pastry. This will keep for a few hours before the puff loses its crunch, but it's best to serve it immediately.

Classic Crème Caramel

For me, this is hands down the best dessert on the planet. I might have, on occasion, eaten a serve intended for six in one sitting. I've used my mum's recipe for aeons, then discovered that a traditional crème caramel uses milk only, no cream, which results in an even lighter, silkier custard. My biggest tip would be to make sure you take your caramel to a deep mahogany, so each mouthful of the sweet custard is accompanied by a beguiling hint of bitterness.

FEEDS 8

CARAMEL
220 g (7¾ oz/1 cup) sugar
60 ml (2 fl oz/¼ cup) water

CUSTARD
900 ml (32 fl oz/3¾ cups)
    full-cream milk
6 eggs + 2 extra yolks
140 g (5 oz/⅔ cup) sugar
1½ teaspoons vanilla bean paste
    OR vanilla extract

METHOD
Before starting, have a 20 cm (8 inch) round cake tin on standby.

To make the caramel, boil the sugar and water in a small stainless steel saucepan until the caramel turns a pale gold. At this stage, watch closely, as it will turn from a rich golden brown to smoking black within seconds. Remove the caramel from the heat a little before it turns the colour you like because it will keep getting darker very quickly. Immediately tip the caramel into the cake tin, then let the caramel set for about 10 minutes, or until hard.

Meanwhile, preheat the oven to 200°C (400°F) fan-forced.

To make the custard, in a medium saucepan, heat the milk over medium heat until hot but not boiling.

Whisk the eggs, extra yolks, sugar and vanilla bean paste in a large mixing bowl until combined. Whisk the hot milk into the mixture, then pour into the tin through a sieve, to catch any lumps of unwhisked egg. Place a clean cloth of some sort on the bottom of a baking dish with high sides (5–6 cm/2–2½ inches). Pop the tin of crème caramel mixture in it, and fill the baking dish halfway up the side of the tin with hot water.

Reduce the oven temperature to 160°C (315°F) fan-forced, cover the tin with foil and bake for 60 minutes. If you jiggle it, the crème caramel should wobble nicely as a whole; if it ripples under the cooked surface, it means it will be liquid and undercooked inside, and needs to be baked longer. Rest for at least 2 hours, then chill completely before slicing to serve. If you want the caramel to liquefy, letting it sit in the refrigerator overnight will do the trick.

To serve, run a thin paring knife around the side of the tin, with the tip touching the bottom. Place a deep serving plate over the tin and, holding both firmly together, flip the crème caramel onto the plate. It should release easily. Slice and serve in a shallow pool of the caramel.

Langues de Chat – Cats' Tongues

These aren't the prettiest bikkie on the block, but I really couldn't write a baking book and not include them because they are one of the first things I ever attempted to bake. I have a soft spot for these also because they're my Great Aunty Kim's favourites. Crisp, sweet and buttery, they're great for adding a crunchy element to a dessert, but I reckon even more fab with a cup of tea.

MAKES 20–25 BISCUITS

INGREDIENTS

120 g (4¼ oz) unsalted butter, softened
110 g (3¾ oz / ½ cup) caster (superfine) sugar
Generous pinch of salt
Finely grated zest of ½ orange
4 egg whites
130 g (4¾ oz / scant 1 cup) plain (all-purpose) flour, sifted

METHOD

Preheat the oven to 190°C (375°F) fan-forced. Line two or three baking trays with baking paper, and have a rolling pin on standby.

Combine the butter, sugar, salt and zest in a medium mixing bowl, and beat with an electric mixer on high speed until pale and fluffy. Add the egg whites one at a time, beating well between each addition, then add the flour, and stir with a whisk until combined.

Transfer the mixture to a piping bag fitted with a 1 cm (½ inch) round nozzle, and pipe even 7 cm (2¾ inch) lines with 7 cm (2¾ inch) gaps between each one onto the prepared baking trays. (Yes, they will spread like nobody's business, so please heed my advice or you'll wind up with one giant biscuit!) Bake for 5–10 minutes until the edges are golden, but the centres still pale.

When cooked, these biscuits can be left on the tray to cool, and they will set flat. If you want them to bend like little cat's tongues, however, you must move very quickly once they are out of the oven. Take out each tray as you need it (because the biscuits will stay malleable when warm), and use a spatula with a thin edge to scoop up the biscuits and drape them over the rolling pin. If you aren't quick enough, they will set and shatter when you try to bend them. Cool completely on a wire rack, before storing in an airtight container for up to 2 weeks.

Quince Clafoutis

For a long time, these fuzzy oversized appley-looking things were too mysterious to tackle, but once I discovered that you simply peel and core (like most fruit) they quickly became my favourite thing to poach. When they're in season, I have them on *everything* – yoghurt, toast, ice cream, pancakes. So why not in a clafoutis? I have a soft spot for clafoutis because, amongst all the baking I've done over the years, it remains one of the most undemanding yet impressive desserts to make. Apart from browning the butter, you can combine the ingredients quite carelessly and still come up trumps. A winner for the self-confessed dud bakers out there.

FEEDS 8–10

POACHED QUINCES

2–3 large quinces, peeled, cored &
    cut into 2 cm (¾ inch) dice
90–150 g (3¼–5½ oz/½–¾ cup)
    caster (superfine) sugar
Enough water to just cover the fruit

BATTER

80 g (2¾ oz) butter
100 g (3½ oz/⅔ cup) plain
    (all-purpose) flour
4 large eggs
110 g (3¾ oz/½ cup) caster
    (superfine) sugar + extra,
    for sprinkling
150 ml (5 fl oz) thin (pouring) cream
150 ml (5 fl oz) milk
1 teaspoon vanilla extract OR
    vanilla essence
⅛ teaspoon salt
2 tablespoons Cointreau OR
    Grand Marnier liqueur
Finely grated zest of 1 orange
    OR lemon

TO SERVE

1 quantity Crème Chantilly
    OR Vanilla Sour Cream OR Vanilla
    Crème Fraîche (for all three,
    see page 203)

METHOD

To poach the quinces, combine the diced fruit, sugar and water in a medium–large saucepan. Bring to the boil over high heat, then reduce the heat and simmer, covered, on the lowest heat possible for 45 minutes until the quinces are tender and pink. (If you want to achieve that gorgeous ruby red, the quinces need another 30 minutes.) Set aside.

Preheat the oven to 180°C (350°F) fan-forced. Brush an ovenproof dish with a 1 litre (35 fl oz/4 cup) capacity and 4–5 cm (1¾–2 inches) deep with softened or melted butter. Coat with caster sugar, then shake out any excess.

To make the batter, melt the butter in a small saucepan over medium heat, and cook until it foams and turns brown. Remove from the heat, and set aside.

Combine the flour, eggs, 110 g (3¾ oz/½ cup) sugar, cream, milk, vanilla, salt, Cointreau and orange zest in a medium mixing bowl. Whisk until smooth. Add the browned butter, and whisk until combined. Drain the quinces in a sieve, then add them to the batter. Stir, then pour into the prepared ovenproof dish. Sprinkle a few tablespoons of caster sugar evenly over the surface of the batter.

Bake for about 35 minutes until a golden brown crust forms on top. Serve with your choice of dolloping cream.

chapter four

SWEETIE PIES & TANTALISING TARTS

Ballerina Mousse & Meringue Tarts

A pillowy raspberry mousse and ethereal meringue, cupped in a crisp orange and almond pâte sablée shell. How you choose to assemble the elements is up to you. The directions I've given you in the recipe are the easiest way, but here I've piped the meringue in a ring and torched it first, then filled the centre with the raspberry mousse.

MAKES ABOUT 10 SMALL TARTS

INGREDIENTS

Plain (all-purpose) flour, for dusting
1 quantity Almond Pâte Sablée
    (see page 209)
1 quantity Italian meringue
    (see page 211)
1 heaped tablespoon dried shredded
    coconut, toasted (optional)

RASPBERRY MOUSSE

150 ml (5 fl oz) milk
3 g (⅛ oz) gelatine sheets
3 egg yolks
85 g (3 oz) caster (superfine) sugar
125 ml (4 fl oz/½ cup)
    raspberry purée
175 ml (5½ fl oz) thickened
    (whipping) cream

RASPBERRY COULIS
(OPTIONAL)

60 g (2¼ oz/¼ cup) fresh OR
    frozen raspberries
2 tablespoons caster
    (superfine) sugar

METHOD

Preheat the oven to 180°C (350°F) fan-forced.

On a lightly floured work surface, roll out the pastry until 3 mm (⅛ inch) thick. Cut 8 cm (3¼ inch) circles with a pastry cutter, and use them to line 5–6 cm (2–2¼ inch) (base diameter) tartlet tins with removable bases. You will end up with about 10 tart shells. If the pastry cracks, don't worry. Squish it back together, and it will bake out. Pierce the base of each one a few times with a fork. Bake for 15–20 minutes until golden. If there are any bubbles when the pastry comes out of the oven, press down gently with a clean oven mitt to flatten.

To make the raspberry mousse, microwave the milk in a heatproof bowl for about 1 minute on the highest setting. Meanwhile, in a medium bowl, soak the gelatine sheets in cool water. Next, whisk the egg yolks and caster sugar in a medium mixing bowl until pale and thick, then add the raspberry purée and whisk to combine. Pour the raspberry mixture into the hot milk, and whisk to combine. Microwave for 2 minutes, and whisk again. The custard will be getting thicker. If not, microwave for 1 minute at a time, whisking well in between, until it easily coats the back of a wooden spoon. Squeeze the water out of the gelatine sheets, then whisk into the custard mixture until dissolved and combined. Press plastic wrap directly onto the surface, and refrigerate for about 45 minutes until cooled and beginning to set. Whisk the cream to soft peaks, and fold through the half-set mixture. Refrigerate until needed.

To make the raspberry coulis, combine the raspberries and sugar in a small saucepan. Stir and bring to the boil, then purée in a blender. Cool completely, before transferring to a piping bag with a 3 mm (⅛ inch) hole snipped off the tip.

To assemble the tarts, transfer the raspberry mousse to a piping bag. If it's a little stiff, whisk very briefly to loosen first. Pipe enough of a blob to fill each tart shell almost to the brim. Pipe a squiggle of the raspberry coulis over this, then sprinkle some toasted coconut on top (if you like). Transfer the Italian meringue to another piping bag fitted with a 1.5–2 cm (⅝–¾ inch) star nozzle. Pipe a swirl to cover the mousse, then torch the meringue well. You want that lovely toasty flavour for contrast against the sweet meringue.

Banana Caramel Cream Pie

You don't eat, you scarf banana caramel pie, Cookie Monster–style, and it seems almost impossible to have only one piece. It's also one of the simplest pies to make, but you do need time for the caramel to develop in the oven. If you prefer, one quantity of the Almond or Chocolate Pâte Sablée (see page 200) works very well to replace the biscuit crumb base.

FEEDS UP TO 12

INGREDIENTS

1 x 395 g (14 oz) tin condensed milk
4 bananas
1 quantity Crème Chantilly, whisked
   to medium peaks (see page 203)

BISCUIT CRUMB BASE

250 g (9 oz) digestive biscuits
   (graham crackers)
120 g (4¼ oz) butter, melted
½ teaspoon ground cinnamon OR
   1 teaspoon finely grated orange
   zest (optional)

METHOD

Preheat the oven to 180°C (350°F) fan-forced.

To make the caramel, pour the condensed milk into a 20 cm (8 inch) round ovenproof dish. Place the dish of condensed milk in a larger baking tin with high sides, and fill the tin with hot water until it comes halfway up the side of the ovenproof dish. Cover with foil, and bake for about 1 hour until the colour of milk chocolate. Set aside to cool completely before using.

Meanwhile, to make the biscuit crumb base, combine the biscuits, butter and cinnamon in a food processor, and pulse until you have a fine crumb. Press evenly and carefully over the bottom and side of a 23–25 cm (9–10 inch) pie dish.

To assemble the pie, spread the caramel evenly over the biscuit crumb base. Peel the bananas, cut into slices 5 mm (¼ inch) thick and arrange over the top of the caramel. Dollop the Crème Chantilly over the bananas, slice and serve.

Marbled Chocolate Salted Caramel Peanut Tart

Think a grown-up Snickers or Picnic when you bite into a piece of this. The feeling is sentimental and familiar, like reuniting with an old mate. It's up to you whether you want to make one large tart or several smaller tarts. Individual tarts will be a bit more fiddly, but the amounts and cooking times stay the same.

FEEDS 12

INGREDIENTS

1 quantity Chocolate Pâte Sablée
 (see page 209)
70 g (2½ oz/½ cup) salted roasted
 peanuts, chopped
1 quantity Milk Chocolate Ganache
 (see page 202)

SALTED CARAMEL

75 g (2½ oz) unsalted butter
50 g (1¾ oz) soft brown sugar
50 g (1¾ oz) caster (superfine) sugar
50 g (1¾ oz) golden syrup (light
 treacle) OR dark corn syrup
125 ml (4 fl oz/½ cup) thickened
 (whipping) cream
½ teaspoon salt OR to taste

DARK CHOCOLATE GANACHE

180 ml (6 fl oz/¾ cup) thickened
 (whipping) cream
180 g (6 oz/1¼ cups) good-quality
 dark chocolate melts (buttons)
 OR chopped dark chocolate
 (70% cocoa solids is best)
⅛ teaspoon salt

TO SERVE

1 quantity Crème Chantilly OR
 Vanilla Sour Cream OR Vanilla
 Crème Fraîche (for all three,
 see page 203)

METHOD

Preheat the oven to 180°C (350°F) fan-forced.

Prepare the tart shell first. On a lightly floured work surface, roll out the pastry into a 32 cm (13 inch) circle, 4 mm (³⁄₁₆ inch) thick. Lower carefully into a 28 cm (11¼ inch) round tart tin with a 3 cm (1¼ inch) high side and a removable bottom. For individual tartlets, roll out until 3 mm (⅛ inch) thick and cut according to the shape and size of the tins. Don't worry if the pastry cracks. Simply squish it back together to seal, and it will bake out. Make sure you press well into the corners. Pinch the excess pastry away, then pierce the base of the pastry shell at regular intervals with a fork.

Blind-bake for 20 minutes. If there are any bubbles when the pastry comes out of the oven, immediately press down gently with a clean oven mitt to deflate and flatten.

To make the salted caramel, combine the butter, brown and caster sugars, golden syrup, cream and salt in a medium saucepan, and bring to the boil. Stir to make sure the sugar has dispersed and dissolved, then simmer for another 5 minutes. Allow to cool completely before using. Spread or pipe evenly to cover the bottom of the tart shell. Sprinkle the peanuts evenly over the salted caramel. Set aside.

To make the dark chocolate ganache, follow the method on page 202 and stir in the salt at the end, then transfer to a piping bag with a 5 mm (¼ inch) hole snipped off the tip. Pipe evenly over the caramel and peanuts.

Transfer the milk chocolate ganache to a piping bag, also with a 5 mm (¼ inch) hole snipped off the tip. Pipe the milk chocolate ganache in lines over the dark chocolate ganache, leaving a 5–10 mm (¼–½ inch) gap between each line. Use a skewer or the tip of a paring knife to drag perpendicular lines across the surface of the ganache, alternating directions so that you get a feathered effect. Allow the ganache to set before slicing. Serve the tart with your choice of dolloping cream.

MARBLED CHOCOLATE SALTED
CARAMEL PEANUT TART

Pecan Pie

Mum used to make a very simple version of this which was, well, all about the pecans and, because this is how I grew up knowing and loving pecan pie to be, anything that deviates from my childhood memory of it is sacrilege. Unfortunately we can't seem to find the original recipe, but this one comes pretty close!

FEEDS 12–14

INGREDIENTS
Plain (all-purpose) flour, for dusting
1 quantity Almond Pâte Sablée
    (see page 209)

FILLING
50 g (1¾ oz) butter, melted
235 g (8½ oz/⅔ cup) golden
    syrup (light treacle) OR dark/
    light corn syrup
165 g (5¾ oz/¾ cup) firmly packed
    soft brown sugar
3 eggs
1 teaspoon vanilla extract OR
    vanilla essence
⅛ teaspoon salt
200 g (7 oz/2 cups) pecans, lightly
    toasted (see first paragraph of
    Basic Nut Praline method on
    page 100)

TO SERVE
Vanilla ice cream OR Crème
    Chantilly (see page 203)

METHOD
Preheat the oven to 180°C (350°F) fan-forced.

On a lightly floured work surface, roll out the pastry to a 32 cm (13 inch) circle, 4 mm (³⁄₁₆ inch) thick. Use it to line a 28 cm (11¼ inch) round tart tin with a 3 cm (1¼ inch) high side and a removable bottom. If the pastry cracks, don't worry. Squish it back together, and it will bake out. Make sure you press well into the corners. Pinch the excess pastry away, then pierce the base of the pastry shell at regular intervals with a fork.

Blind-bake for about 20 minutes until golden. If there are any bubbles when the pastry comes out of the oven, immediately press down gently with a clean oven mitt to deflate and flatten. Leave the oven on.

Meanwhile, to make the filling, combine the butter, golden syrup, brown sugar, eggs, vanilla and salt in a medium mixing bowl, and whisk until smooth. Stir in the nuts, then pour into the tart shell and bake for another 20 minutes until the centre is no longer wobbly. Cool completely, before cutting and serving with ice cream or Crème Chantilly.

Prune Custard Tart

This very French combination of prunes, custard and pastry is a fab example of restraint and elegance with simplicity at the core of its philosophy.

FEEDS 12–14

INGREDIENTS
Plain (all-purpose) flour, for dusting
1 quantity Almond Pâte Sablée
   (see page 209)
1 quantity prune purée
   (see Prune and Armagnac
   Breton, page 69)

CUSTARD
350 ml (12 fl oz) milk
4 eggs
150 g (5½ oz/⅔ cup) caster
   (superfine) sugar
1½ teaspoons vanilla extract
2 tablespoons wheaten cornflour
   (cornstarch), see note on
   page 33

METHOD
Preheat the oven to 180°C (350°F) fan-forced.

On a lightly floured work surface, roll out the pastry to a 32 cm (13 inch) circle, 4 mm (³⁄₁₆ inch) thick. Use it to line a 28 cm (11¼ inch) round tart tin with a 3 cm (1¼ inch) high side and a removable bottom. If the pastry cracks, don't worry. Squish it back together, and it will bake out. Make sure you press well into the corners. Pinch the excess pastry away, then pierce the base of the pastry shell at regular intervals with a fork.

Blind-bake for about 20 minutes until golden. If there are any bubbles when the pastry comes out of the oven, immediately press down gently with a clean oven mitt, to deflate and flatten. Do not turn off the oven.

To make the custard, microwave the milk in a heatproof bowl for 1½ minutes on the highest setting. Meanwhile, whisk together the eggs, sugar and vanilla in a medium mixing bowl until pale and thick. Add the cornflour, and whisk until smooth. Pour this mixture into the hot milk, and whisk to combine. Buzz in the microwave for 2 minutes on the highest setting. Whisk until smooth, then microwave in 1-minute bursts until the mixture forms a thick paste.

Spread the prune purée evenly over the base of the tart shell. Pour the custard on top, and smooth the surface with a spatula or knife. Bake for about 20 minutes until the tart shell is golden brown and the custard set. Cool completely, before slicing and serving.

Blueberry Bakewell Tart

This British favourite is essentially a shortcrust pastry filled with a layer of jam and frangipane. It's not customary to use fruit as well, but it's nice for bolstering the flavour of the jam and adding textural interest. Of course, use any flavour jam you like – here I'm using blueberry, but my other fave is cherry jam and sour (morello) cherries. You can also use hazelnut meal instead of almond, if you want to cause a scene and not adhere to 'Bakewell' conventions.

FEEDS 12

INGREDIENTS

1 quantity Almond Pâte Sablée (see page 209)

115 g (4 oz/⅓ cup) blueberry jam

80 g (2¾ oz/½ cup) fresh OR thawed frozen blueberries, well drained

50 g (1¾ oz) flaked almonds

FRANGIPANE FILLING

125 g (4½ oz) unsalted butter, softened

125 g (4½ oz) caster (superfine) sugar

¼ teaspoon salt

½ teaspoon almond extract OR 1 teaspoon grated lemon zest OR orange zest

2 large eggs

100 g (3½ oz/1 cup) almond meal, sifted

30 g (1 oz) plain (all-purpose) flour, sifted + extra, for dusting

ICING

80 g (2¾ oz/⅔ cup) icing (confectioners') sugar, sifted

2½ teaspoons water

TO SERVE

1 quantity Crème Chantilly OR Vanilla Sour Cream (for both, see page 203) OR Yoghurt Mascarpone Cream (see page 206)

METHOD

Preheat the oven to 180°C (350°F) fan-forced.

On a lightly floured work surface, roll out the pastry into a 32 cm (13 inch) circle, 4 mm (³⁄₁₆ inch) thick. Use it to line a 28 cm (11¼ inch) round tart tin with a 3 cm (1¼ inch) high side and a removable bottom. Don't worry if the pastry cracks. Simply squish it back together, and it will bake out. Make sure you press well into the corners. Pinch the excess pastry away, then pierce the base of the pastry shell at regular intervals with a fork.

Blind-bake for about 20 minutes until pale golden. If there are any bubbles when the pastry comes out of the oven, immediately press down gently with a clean oven mitt, to deflate and flatten. Do not turn off the oven.

Allow the tart shell to cool a little, before spreading the jam evenly over the base.

To make the frangipane filling, combine the butter, sugar, salt and almond extract in a medium mixing bowl, and beat with an electric mixer on the highest setting until pale and fluffy. Add the eggs one at a time, beating well between each addition. Fold in the almond meal and plain flour. Spread the mixture smoothly over the jam, then dot the surface evenly with the blueberries, gently pressing them into the mixture. Sprinkle all over with the flaked almonds.

Bake for 40 minutes, or until an inserted skewer comes out clean. Cool completely before icing.

To make the icing, combine the icing sugar with the water in a medium mixing bowl, and whisk until smooth. Transfer the mixture to a piping bag with a 2 mm (¹⁄₁₆ inch) hole snipped off the tip, then pipe a zigzag pattern across the surface of the tart. Serve with your choice of dolloping cream.

White Chocolate Ganache Raspberry Tart

I've always steered away from this well-loved combo of white chocolate and raspberries because of its cloying sweetness, but add a little kick of sharpness with crème fraîche and it's transformed. As with all the tarts in this book, you may choose to make smaller individual tartlets as I have, or one large tart.

MAKES ABOUT 12 INDIVIDUAL TARTS OR 1 LARGE TART

INGREDIENTS
Plain (all-purpose) flour, for dusting
1 quantity Almond Pâte Sablée
    (see page 209)

RASPBERRY COULIS
350 g (12 oz) frozen OR fresh
    raspberries
75 g (2½ oz/⅓ cup) caster
    (superfine) sugar

WHITE CHOCOLATE GANACHE
200 g (7 oz) thickened
    (whipping) cream
400 g (14 oz) white chocolate melts
    (buttons) OR roughly chopped
    white chocolate
⅛ teaspoon salt

TO SERVE
250 ml (9 fl oz/1 cup) crème fraîche
    OR sour cream

METHOD
Preheat the oven to 170°C (325°F) fan-forced.

On a lightly floured work surface, roll out the pastry into a 32 cm (13 inch) circle, 4 mm (³⁄₁₆ inch) thick. Use it to line a 28 cm (11¼ inch) round tart tin with a 3 cm (1¼ inch) high side and a removable bottom. For individual tartlets, roll out the pastry until 3 mm (⅛ inch) thick, and cut according to the shape and size of the tins. If the pastry cracks, don't worry. Squish it back together, and it will bake out. Make sure you press well into the corners. Pinch the excess pastry away, then pierce the base of the pastry shell at regular intervals with a fork.

Blind-bake for about 20 minutes until golden. If there are any bubbles when the pastry comes out of the oven, immediately press down gently with a clean oven mitt to deflate and flatten.

To make the raspberry coulis, combine the raspberries and sugar in a small saucepan, and bring to the boil. Stir until the sugar has dissolved, then purée with a blender. Cover and refrigerate.

To make the ganache, microwave the cream, white chocolate and salt in a medium heatproof bowl for 1½ minutes on the highest setting. Whisk until smooth. Allow to rest for 10 minutes, so the ganache is not quite so runny.

To assemble, spoon in enough raspberry coulis to coat the bottom of each tart shell well. Alternatively, you can pipe the coulis on top of the ganache after it has set – it's very much up to you how you want to assemble the elements. Spoon the ganache into each tart shell to about 1 cm (½ inch) deep, and refrigerate for about 15 minutes. Place a scoop of crème fraîche on top of each tart. If making a single large tart, slice and serve immediately with the crème fraîche for dolloping.

Baked Lime & Chocolate Tart

If you're going for citrus as your headliner, it has to be legit. By this, I mean sharp with tons of zest; alive and punchy. Otherwise, why bother? And for contrast, the smoky, biscuity Chocolate Pâte Sablée couldn't be more perfect. This one's a keeper!

FEEDS UP TO 12

INGREDIENTS
Plain (all-purpose) flour, for dusting
1 quantity Chocolate Pâte Sablée
   (see page 209)

FILLING
5 eggs
250 ml (9 fl oz/1 cup) thickened
   (whipping) cream
165 g (5¾ oz/¾ cup) caster
   (superfine) sugar
Grated zest of 4–5 limes
125 ml (4 fl oz/½ cup) lime juice
A few drops of green food colouring

TO SERVE
1 quantity Crème Chantilly
   (see page 203)

METHOD
Preheat the oven to 180°C (350°F) fan-forced.

On a lightly floured work surface, roll out the pastry into a 32 cm (13 inch) circle, 4 mm (³⁄₁₆ inch) thick. Use it to line a 28 cm (11¼ inch) round tart tin with a 3 cm (1¼ inch) high side and a removable bottom. Don't worry if the pastry cracks. Simply squish it back together, and it will bake out. Make sure you press well into the corners. Pinch the excess pastry away, then pierce the base of the tart shell at regular intervals with a fork.

Blind-bake for 20 minutes. If there are any bubbles when the pastry comes out of the oven, immediately press down gently with a clean oven mitt, to deflate and flatten. Set aside in its tin.

To make the filling, combine the eggs, cream, sugar, lime zest and juice in a medium mixing bowl, and whisk until combined. Add enough food colouring to tint the mixture the palest shade of green. Place the baked tart shell (still in its tin) on a baking tray. Pour the filling mixture into the tart shell, then reduce the oven temperature to 160°C (315°F) fan-forced, and bake for 30 minutes until just set. Cool completely before chilling. Slice and serve with the Crème Chantilly.

chapter five

OLDIES BUT GOODIES

Basic Nut Praline

I'm not going to lie. These are dangerously moreish – possibly my favourite holiday-season snack. You can use praline for desserts, but I like to crack these deep amber pools of nut-studded goodness into generous-sized shards and wrap them in cellophane to make stunning Christmas gifts. Warning! Do *not* refrigerate, or the caramel will turn into a liquid, sticky mess. Keep in an airtight container at room temperature.

MAKES ABOUT 650 G (1 LB 7 OZ) OF PRALINE

INGREDIENTS

500 g (1 lb 2 oz) of your favourite nuts (choose the freshest ones possible)

150 g (5½ oz) caster (superfine) sugar

3 tablespoons water

METHOD

Preheat the oven to 180°C (350°F) fan-forced (see note below).

Spread out the nuts in a single layer on a baking tray. Roast in the oven for 10–15 minutes, or until deep golden. If skins are on hazelnuts, they should be flaking off. Shake the nuts in a colander with large holes to be rid of the skins. Otherwise, tip them into a clean tea towel, and rub gently to remove the skins. Roughly chop any larger nuts such as macadamias. Scatter the roasted nuts on a baking tray lined with baking paper – make sure they aren't spaced too far apart or you'll get really large areas of caramel that will become jaw-breakers!

To make the caramel, combine the sugar and water in a non-stick, heavy-based saucepan. Stir to dissolve a little, then do *not* stir the mixture again. Boil over high heat until the caramel turns a pale golden colour. At this stage, watch closely, as it will turn from an ideal rich golden brown to smoking black within seconds – although using a non-stick pot will slow things down a little.

Remove the caramel from the heat a little before it turns the colour you like because it will keep getting darker very quickly. Immediately pour the caramel over the nuts. Allow to set completely, before breaking into large shards.

If you want to use the praline for a bit of crunch and bitterness in a dessert, chop into a coarse crumb or pound very softly using a mortar and pestle, to avoid the caramel compressing into a dense, sticky clump.

NOTE

For finer, processed nuts such as slivered or flaked almonds, or pine nuts, reduce the oven temperature to 160°C (320°F) fan-forced. Roast for 7 minutes or until golden brown.

Pecan Cinnamon Scrolls

This old favourite is perfect for an after-school treat, and guaranteed to be greeted with enthusiasm. Make the dough in your PJs the night before, then the next day set your kids free in the kitchen to finish off the job. It's a win–win!

MAKES 8 LARGE SCROLLS

DOUGH
450 g (1 lb/3 cups) plain (all-purpose) flour + extra, for dusting
2 teaspoons dried yeast
1 tablespoon caster (superfine) sugar
250 ml (9 fl oz/1 cup) tepid milk
1 egg
½ teaspoon salt

SCROLL FILLING
80 g (2¾ oz) butter, softened
110 g (3¾ oz/½ cup firmly packed) soft brown sugar
2 teaspoons ground cinnamon
90 g (3¼ oz/¾ cup) toasted pecans, finely chopped (see first paragraph of method on opposite page)

MAPLE GLAZE
60 g (2¼ oz/½ cup) pure icing (confectioners') sugar
2 tablespoons maple syrup

METHOD

To make the dough, combine the flour, yeast, sugar, milk and egg in the bowl of an electric stand mixer fitted with the hook attachment. Hook on the lowest speed for 1 minute, then add the salt and hook for another minute until smooth and elastic. Knead the dough briefly on a very lightly floured work surface, and shape into a disc. Rest on a plate lined with baking paper, then cover with plastic wrap and refrigerate overnight.

The next day, turn the base of a 24–25 cm (9½–10 inch) springform tin upside down, so it no longer has a lip. Place a piece of baking paper over the base, then clamp the ring around it to secure. Grease the ring, then cut strips of baking paper to line the side.

To make the scroll filling, combine the butter, brown sugar and cinnamon in a medium mixing bowl, and rub until the crumb has a sandy texture. Add the nuts, and mix until combined.

On a lightly floured work surface, roll out the dough into a 40 x 30 cm (16 x 12 inch) rectangle. Spread the filling evenly over the dough, leaving a 2 cm (¾ inch) border. Roll this as snugly as possible, with the longest side forming the length of the log. Cut into eight equal slices, and space them evenly in the tin with the spiral/scroll pattern facing upwards. Allow the scrolls to rest in a draught-free spot in the house – and a warm one if possible – until they have doubled in size (1–3 hours, depending on the weather).

Preheat the oven to 200°C (400°F) fan-forced.

Bake the cinnamon scrolls for 10 minutes, then reduce the oven temperature to 170°C (325°F) fan-forced and bake for another 30 minutes. (If the scrolls are browning too quickly, place some foil over them.) Allow the scrolls to cool briefly, before releasing them from the tin and turning out onto a wire rack. Cool completely before glazing.

To make the maple glaze, mix the icing sugar with the maple syrup and a little water until you have a smooth, runny consistency, then drizzle over the scrolls with a spoon or pipe in a zigzag pattern using a piping bag with a small hole snipped off the tip.

PECAN CINNAMON SCROLLS

Forever Coconut Ice

Just because something's retro, doesn't mean it's no longer awesome! Mum had these on tap when we were growing up, so the stuff seeps through my veins. And there are so many pluses – cheap, quick and *so* delicious. They're great on a party table, but they also make simple gifts, easily prettied up for the holiday season.

MAKES ABOUT 160 PIECES

INGREDIENTS

270 g (9½ oz/3 cups) desiccated OR dried shredded coconut

2 tablespoons hot water

250 ml (9 fl oz/1 cup) evaporated milk

550 g (1 lb 4 oz/2½ cups) caster (superfine) sugar

3 tablespoons butter

¼ teaspoon salt

A few drops of red food colouring

METHOD

Line the bottom of a 20 x 25 cm (8 x 10 inch) baking dish or baking tin, and grease the sides.

Combine the coconut and hot water in a medium non-stick saucepan, and stir until the water has been absorbed. Add the remaining ingredients, and stir to combine. Cook over medium heat until the sugar has dissolved and the mixture leaves the side of the saucepan.

Press evenly into the prepared baking dish, and allow to cool completely, before turning it out and slicing into 2 cm (¾ inch) squares. These keep for up to 3 weeks in an airtight container.

Ann's Cherry Ripe

My late mother-in-law, Ann, was a loving, spirited woman who raised six strong children on the sniff of an oily rag. She made no secret of her basic cooking and eating repertoires, but her one true weakness was chocolate, and this old favourite was one of the things she was known for. The brilliant thing, of course, is that it takes very few ingredients and just a few blinks to put together, but tastes a close second to the real thing! A great one for a homemade lunchbox treat.

MAKES 12 LARGE BARS OR 24 BITE-SIZED PIECES

INGREDIENTS

250 g (9 oz) dark chocolate melts (buttons) OR chopped dark chocolate
2 eggs
110 g (3¾ oz/½ cup) caster (superfine) sugar
90 g (3¼ oz/1 cup) desiccated OR dried shredded coconut
100 g (3½ oz) glacé cherries, finely chopped

METHOD

Preheat the oven to 170°C (325°F) fan-forced. Line a 20 cm (8 inch) square cake tin with baking paper.

Microwave the chocolate in a heatproof bowl for 1 minute on the highest setting. Whisk or stir with a spoon, then see whether the chocolate needs more melting. If so, buzz for another 30 seconds, but be careful not to overcook it or the chocolate will seize. The other way is to use the double-boiler method: pop the chocolate in a heatproof bowl, and sit it on a saucepan filled with about 3 cm (1¼ inch) of simmering water. Stir until the chocolate has melted.

Spread the chocolate evenly over the bottom of the prepared tin. Set in the refrigerator.

Meanwhile, combine the eggs and sugar in a medium mixing bowl, and whisk until pale and thick. Fold in the coconut and cherries, spread evenly over the chocolate and bake for 10–15 minutes until the coconut is slightly golden. Cool in the tin, then chill completely before cutting into bars or squares for eating.

Any Muffin with Oat & Cinnamon Crumble

'Any muffin' because you can use it as a base with whatever fruit you like and it will turn out ace. It's a great one for lunchboxes or a quick brekky, and very user-friendly for kids who are dying to help in the kitchen because it almost needs to be stirred carelessly, until barely combined, for the lightest result. The sour cream keeps the muffin gorgeously moist, and the crumble jazzes things up with a bit of crunch.

MAKES 10–12 MUFFINS

INGREDIENTS

300 g (10½ oz/2 cups) plain (all-purpose) flour, sifted

3 teaspoons baking powder, sifted

½ teaspoon salt

220 g (7¾ oz/1 cup firmly packed) soft brown sugar

90 g (3¼ oz) unsalted butter, melted

1 egg, lightly whisked

125 ml (4 fl oz/½ cup) milk

80 ml (2½ fl oz/⅓ cup) sour cream

1 teaspoon vanilla extract OR vanilla essence

About 200 g (7 oz/1½ cups) fresh OR frozen berries OR any fresh OR cooled stewed fruit, cut into 1 cm (½ inch) dice

OAT & CINNAMON CRUMBLE

50 g (1¾ oz/⅓ cup) plain (all-purpose) flour

50 g (1¾ oz/½ cup) rolled oats

30 g (1 oz) soft brown sugar

½ teaspoon ground cinnamon

50 g (1¾ oz) chilled unsalted butter, cubed

60 g (2 oz/½ cup) chopped nuts of choice

METHOD

Preheat the oven to 170°C (325°F) fan-forced. Line a 12-hole standard muffin tin with paper cases.

To make the crumble, blitz the flour, oats, brown sugar, cinnamon and butter in a food processor to a sticky, sandy consistency. If doing it by hand, chop the butter finely, and rub into the dry ingredients until there are no big chunks of butter, but instead a fine, crumbly consistency. Stir the nuts into the crumble. Refrigerate until needed.

To make the muffin batter, combine the flour, baking powder, salt and brown sugar in a medium mixing bowl. Whisk briefly to mix the dry ingredients. Add the melted butter, egg, milk, sour cream, vanilla and the stewed fruit, and mix with a wooden spoon until just combined. Fill the prepared paper cases until three-quarters full, then sprinkle a tablespoonful of the crumble over each one.

Bake for about 15 minutes, or until an inserted skewer comes out clean. Allow the muffins to cool in the tin for about 5 minutes, before moving to a wire rack and cooling completely.

Apricot Granola

Hands down the best granola you will ever make and taste. Funk it up with different purées, nuts, seeds and dried fruit. Just make sure you toast all the ingredients until they're the deepest golden brown, and you will never buy this from the store again. Ever.

MAKES ABOUT 1.6 KG (3½ LB)

INGREDIENTS

450 g (1 lb/4½ cups) rolled oats
120 g (4¼ oz/¾ cup) sunflower seeds
120 g (4¼ oz/¾ cup) sesame seeds
100 g (3½ oz/½ cup lightly packed) soft brown sugar
250 g (9 oz/1½ cups) whole natural almonds, roughly chopped, some left whole
2 teaspoons ground cinnamon
1 teaspoon ground ginger
1 teaspoon sea salt flakes
120 g (4½ oz/⅓ cup) golden syrup (light treacle) OR dark corn syrup
4 tablespoons honey
170 g (6 oz) apricot nectar (purée) OR any other fruit purée
2 tablespoons grapeseed oil
100 g (3½ oz/1½ cups) dried shredded coconut
280 g (10 oz/1¾ cups) chopped dried apricots OR other dried fruit of choice

METHOD

Preheat the oven to 170°C (325°F) fan-forced. Line a large baking tray with baking paper.

Using clean hands, mix the rolled oats, sunflower seeds, sesame seeds, brown sugar, almonds, cinnamon, ginger and salt in a large bowl. Add the golden syrup, honey, apricot nectar and oil, and mix well. Spread the mixture evenly over the prepared tray, and bake for 20 minutes. Add the coconut, and mix well using a spatula. Spread out the mixture evenly again, and bake for another 10 minutes until deep golden brown.

Remove the tray from the oven, and sprinkle the dried apricots evenly over the granola. Mix through, then allow to cool completely before storing in an airtight container. Great as a gift and keeps for a month.

Chocolate Sherry Log

I have many memories of Mum making this when we first migrated to Australia – *the* amazing no-bake cake! When Jono and I were married in Penguin, Tasmania, two years ago, I wanted everything to be fuss-free because my mother-in-law, Ann, was very unwell. Seeing as this was also something Ann used to make, I thought it would be great fun for each family member to make sections of this into the shape of a heart. The end result was more heart shape 'inspired', but I'm certain it remains the most endearing wedding cake ever made.

FEEDS ABOUT 10

INGREDIENTS

500 ml (17 fl oz/2 cups) thickened (whipping) cream
50 g (1¾ oz) icing (confectioners') sugar
1 teaspoon vanilla extract OR vanilla essence
250–500 ml (9–17 fl oz/1–2 cups) sweet sherry OR any liqueur (Frangelico or kirsch is very nice)
1 packet chocolate-flavoured biscuits (cookies) such as chocolate ripple
50 g (1¾ oz/½ cup) toasted flaked almonds (see note on page 100)

METHOD

Whisk the cream, icing sugar and vanilla in a medium mixing bowl until stiff peaks form. Pour the sherry into a separate bowl, and have your serving plate ready – a long, rectangular one is ideal for the log.

Begin by roughly spreading a line of cream along the centre of the serving plate, on which to form the log. Dip a biscuit in the sherry, then spread about a teaspoonful of cream on it. Repeat the process, sandwiching the biscuits together until you cover the length of the platter or run out of biscuits.

Spread more cream over the entire surface of the log, then cover with the flaked almonds. Cover with plastic wrap, and chill for a minimum of 5 hours or overnight before serving. Cut on a diagonal to serve.

Lazy Daisy Apple Turnovers

If you are the cruddiest dessert cook in the world, this is your guy. Quick, easy and a major crowd-pleaser.

MAKES 4 TURNOVERS

INGREDIENTS

2 x 20 cm (8 inch) square sheets ready-made butter puff pastry OR 1 quantity homemade Rough Puff Pastry (see page 200)
2 pink lady OR granny smith apples
4 tablespoons soft brown sugar
4 small pinches of salt
Ground cinnamon, to taste
60 g (2¼ oz) unsalted butter, sliced into 4 thin sheets
1 egg, whisked, for egg wash
4 heaped tablespoons raw (demerara) sugar

TO SERVE

Vanilla ice cream OR ½ quantity Crème Chantilly (see page 203)

METHOD

Preheat the oven to 190°C (375°F) fan-forced. Grease a baking tray well.

Slice each sheet of puff pastry in half, so you have four long rectangles. Peel, core and halve the apples, then cut into thin slices. Place half an apple's worth of slices onto one half of each piece of puff, slanting them so they sit as flat as possible. Sprinkle each one with 1 tablespoon of soft brown sugar and a pinch of salt and cinnamon. Top with a thin sheet of butter. Fold the free half of the puff over the apple mixture, and press down the edges with a fork, so that you end up with a squarish apple turnover. Baste with the egg wash, then sprinkle each turnover with 1 heaped tablespoon of the raw sugar.

Bake for about 20 minutes until the pastry is a deep golden brown and beautifully puffed up. Serve warm with vanilla ice cream or Crème Chantilly.

TIP

Puff pastry must be used when still chilled. If it feels and looks like it's wilting, immediately pop it in the refrigerator for 10–15 minutes, then continue to work; otherwise the puff won't rise in the oven.

St Clement's Pud with Lavender Cream

I couldn't choose between a blood orange or a lemon self-saucing pudding, so a non-decision of St Clement's it would be. The faintest perfume of French lavender infused through the cream pushes things up a little, and goes so well with the sharpness of the citrus.

FEEDS UP TO 10

INGREDIENTS

3 eggs, separated
220 g (7¾ oz/1 cup) caster
   (superfine) sugar
60 g (2¼ oz) unsalted butter,
   softened
¼ teaspoon salt
Finely grated zest & juice of 1 lemon
Finely grated zest & juice of 1 blood
   orange OR 1 regular orange
375 ml (13 fl oz/1½ cups) milk
80 g (2¾ oz) self-raising flour

LAVENDER CREAM

250 ml (9 fl oz/1 cup) thickened
   (whipping) cream
½ teaspoon unsprayed dried French
   lavender buds
25 g (1 oz) icing (confectioners')
   sugar
½ teaspoon vanilla bean paste
   OR vanilla extract

METHOD

Preheat the oven to 180°C (350°F) fan-forced. Have a 1 litre (35 fl oz/4 cup) glass or ceramic ovenproof dish on standby.

To make the lavender cream, combine the cream and lavender in a small saucepan over medium heat. Gently heat until hot to the touch, but with no bubbles rising. Remove from the heat, cover and chill.

To make the pudding, place the egg whites in a medium mixing bowl, and whisk with an electric mixer on high speed until soft peaks form. Divide the sugar in half, and add tablespoonsful at a time to the egg whites, beating well between each addition, until half of the sugar has been used and you have medium peaks. Set aside.

Combine the butter, remaining sugar, salt and lemon and orange zests in a medium mixing bowl. Beat with an electric mixer on high speed until pale and fluffy. Add the yolks one at a time, beating well between each addition. Whisk in the milk until smooth, then add the flour and whisk to combine. Add both the juices, and whisk until combined. Don't worry if the mixture curdles. Add the reserved egg whites to the mixture, and stir with a whisk until mixed through.

Pour the mixture into the ovenproof dish, then sit it in a roasting tin. Fill the roasting tin with hot water until it reaches halfway up the side of the ovenproof dish. Bake for 1 hour – there should be a very light cake on top and a velvety custard underneath. If there is no custard, it means you've overcooked it a little, but it will still be yum. Next time, simply reduce the cooking time by about 6 minutes.

Just before serving, pass the chilled lavender-infused cream through a sieve over a medium mixing bowl, to catch then discard the lavender buds. Whisk the cream with the icing sugar and vanilla in a medium mixing bowl until very soft peaks form. Serve a scoop of the pudding with a generous dollop of the lavender cream.

Rum Babas

You won't believe it, but I've only recently discovered this squelchy, rummy gem of a classic. The best way to do a rum baba justice is to eat it plain, but if you prefer more layers of flavour you can serve it with fresh fruit and/or crème Chantilly (see page 203). The savarin recipe was given to me by my late friend Emmanuel Mollois. Savarin dough creates a drier-style brioche, designed to be soaked in syrup.

MAKES ABOUT 12 BABAS

SAVARIN
350 g (12 oz/2⅓ cups) plain
   (all-purpose) flour
50 g (1¾ oz) caster (superfine) sugar
   + extra, for coating moulds
3 teaspoons dried yeast
100 ml (3½ fl oz) tepid milk
4 eggs
Finely grated zest of 1 lemon
¼ teaspoon salt
150 g (5½ oz) butter, softened

RUM SYRUP
300 g (10½ oz) sugar
250 ml (9 fl oz/1 cup) water
185 ml (6 fl oz/¾ cup) rum

TO SERVE
1 quantity chilled Crème Chantilly
   (see page 203) OR
   Yoghurt Mascarpone Cream
   (see page 206) (optional)

METHOD

To make the savarin, combine the flour, caster sugar, yeast, milk, eggs zest and salt in an electric stand mixer fitted with a dough hook attachment. Hook on the lowest speed for about 10 minutes until the dough is smooth and glossy. Add the butter gradually until it has all been used and the dough is very stretchy. Cover with plastic wrap, and rest in a draught-free spot in the house – and a warm one if possible – until it doubles in volume. This can take anywhere from 1–3 hours, depending on the weather.

Preheat the oven to 200°C (400°F) fan-forced. Grease 12 individual baba (dariole) moulds well, then coat them with the extra caster sugar and shake out any excess. If you don't have proper baba moulds, you can grease and sugar a standard muffin tin.

Transfer the savarin to a piping bag, snip a 1.5 cm (⅝ inch) diameter hole off the tip and pipe enough mixture to fill three-quarters of each tin. Allow the dough to rise again until it reaches the top of the moulds and is wobbly when shaken.

Reduce the oven temperature to 180°C (350°F) fan-forced, and bake for about 15 minutes until the babas are beautifully golden. Shake them out of the moulds onto a wire rack as soon as they are out of the oven. Cool completely, before drenching in the syrup.

Meanwhile, to make the syrup, combine the sugar and water in a small saucepan. Stir and bring to the boil, then reduce to a simmer. Simmer for about 2 minutes until the syrup thickens a little, then add the rum and allow to simmer for another 30 seconds. Remove from the heat and lower the babas into the hot syrup using a slotted spoon. Allow them to soak up the syrup, then place them on a wire rack sitting over a baking tray, so the excess syrup can drip away.

Serve the babas warm, with a jug of syrup on the side, or allow to cool completely if you want to serve with your dolloping cream of choice.

Digestive Biscuits

I know. How very nana of me! My favourite way to eat these is with an aged cheddar, but sandwiching them together with a bit of melted dark chocolate or salted caramel, even plain with a cup of tea ... winning!

MAKES ABOUT 24 BISCUITS

INGREDIENTS

150 g (5½ oz) wholemeal (whole-wheat) flour + extra, for dusting

150 g (5½ oz) oatmeal

50 g (1¾ oz) soft brown sugar

1½ teaspoons baking powder

½ teaspoon salt

100 g (3½ oz) chilled unsalted butter, cut into 1 cm (½ inch) dice

2–3 tablespoons milk

METHOD

Preheat the oven to 170°C (325°F) fan-forced. Line two baking trays with baking paper.

Combine all the dry ingredients in a food processor, and pulse very briefly to mix. Add the butter, and pulse until you have a sandy texture. Tip the mixture into a medium mixing bowl, and add only 2 tablespoons of the milk first, then the remainder if the mixture feels a little dry. Patiently squeeze the mixture together until it all binds into a firm dough. Shape the dough into a disc, and flatten to about 1 cm (½ inch) thick. Cover with plastic wrap, and chill for 30 minutes.

Lightly flour your work surface and the top of the dough, then roll out until 3 mm (⅛ inch) thick. Using a 5 cm (2 inch) pastry cutter, cut out circles to make the biscuits. Space them 1 cm (½ inch) apart on the prepared baking trays, and bake for about 15 minutes until golden.

These will keep well for up to 2 weeks in an airtight container.

Bienenstich – Bee Sting Cake

I've eaten Bienenstich for years, not realising it's really just brioche baked in a round cake tin with a caramel nut topping and custard in the middle! I guess that's why it's so important to know the classics because, with these basic skills, so many delicious yet simple things can be made.

FEEDS ABOUT 10

BRIOCHE

260 g (9¼ oz/1¾ cups) plain (all-purpose) flour + extra, for dusting
1 teaspoon dried yeast
2 tablespoons caster (superfine) sugar
25 g (1 oz) unsalted butter, softened
130 ml (4½ fl oz) tepid milk
1 large egg
½ teaspoon salt

TOPPING

50 g (2¼ oz) unsalted butter
55 g (2 oz/¼ cup) caster (superfine) sugar
1 tablespoon milk
1 tablespoon honey
¼ teaspoon salt
80 g (2¾ oz/¾ cup) flaked almonds

TO FINISH

½ quantity chilled Crème Pâtissière (see page 204)
50 ml (1¾ fl oz) thickened (whipping) cream

METHOD

To make the brioche, combine the flour, yeast, sugar, butter, milk and egg in the bowl of an electric stand mixer fitted with a dough hook attachment. Hook on the lowest setting for 2 minutes, then add the salt and hook for a further 5 minutes until the dough is sticky, smooth and glossy. Leave the dough in the bowl, and press plastic wrap directly on its surface, making sure any gaps around the side are sealed. Refrigerate overnight.

The next day, grease the ring of a 22 cm (8½ inch) springform tin with butter, then cut strips of baking paper to line the side. Turn the base of the tin upside down, so it no longer has a lip. Place a piece of baking paper over it, then clamp the ring around it to secure.

Scrape the dough out of the mixing bowl into the prepared tin. Sprinkle some flour over the top to stop your fingers from sticking, and press it evenly to cover the bottom of the tin. Cover with plastic wrap, then a clean tea towel, and allow to rise in a draught-free spot in the house – and a warm one if possible – for about 1 hour, or until the dough has doubled in volume.

Preheat the oven to 180°C (350°F) fan-forced.

To make the topping, combine the butter, caster sugar, milk, honey and salt in a small saucepan. Cook over medium heat until everything has melted and combined. Stir in the nuts, then set aside to cool.

Spread the topping carefully and evenly over the surface of the risen dough, and bake for about 30 minutes, or until an inserted skewer comes out clean. Cool the brioche completely, before removing from the tin.

To finish, place the chilled crème pâtissière in a medium mixing bowl, and whisk with an electric mixer on high speed for about 10 seconds, to loosen the mixture. Add the cream and whisk until combined.

Use a serrated knife to slice the cake in half horizontally, then slice the top half into 12 segments. Otherwise the nuts will shred the brioche on the way down and all the custard will ooze out. Spread the custard on the bottom half, replace the individual top slices, cut all the way through the bottom half and serve. This is best eaten on the day it is baked.

Chewy Apricot & Almond Anzacs

Anzac biscuits are truly one of my old-fashioned favourites, but when I discovered the chewy version my brain just about melted. Take these to your nan's house one afternoon, and you will be immediately crowned 'favourite grandchild'. With a cup of tea, Anzacs are up there as one of those simple things in life that you just can't beat – so delicious and nostalgic.

MAKES ABOUT 24

INGREDIENTS

150 g (5½ oz/1 cup) wholemeal (whole-wheat) OR plain (all-purpose) flour, sifted

95 g (3¼ oz/1 cup) rolled (porridge) oats

65 g (2½ oz/1 cup) dried shredded coconut OR desiccated coconut

235 g (8½ oz/1½ cups) dried apricots, cut into 5 mm (¼ inch) dice

115 g (4 oz/¾ cup) chopped toasted almonds (see first paragraph of Basic Nut Praline method on page 100)

165 g (5¾ oz/¾ cup firmly packed) soft brown sugar

⅛ teaspoon salt

135 g (4¾ oz) unsalted butter

2 tablespoons golden syrup (light treacle)

2½ tablespoons water

1 teaspoon bicarbonate of soda (baking soda)

METHOD

Preheat the oven to 160°C (315°F) fan-forced. Line two baking trays with baking paper.

Combine the flour, oats, coconut, apricots, nuts, sugar and salt in a medium–large mixing bowl. In a small saucepan over medium heat, melt the butter with the golden syrup and water. Stir briefly, then remove from the heat. Add the bicarbonate of soda – this will make the mixture fizz, but don't be worried. Add to the dry mixture, and mix with a wooden spoon (even better with your hands) until the ingredients are well combined.

Roll heaped teaspoons of the mixture into golf ball-sized balls, then press gently with a fork to flatten the biscuits slightly. Space them about 4 cm (1½ inches) apart on the prepared trays. Bake for 10–15 minutes until golden. Let the biscuits rest for 5 minutes on the baking trays, before transferring them to a wire rack to cool – being a chewy-style biscuit, they are a little flimsy when fresh out of the oven and will fall apart if you try to pick them up immediately.

These will keep for up to 2 weeks in an airtight container and also freeze very well.

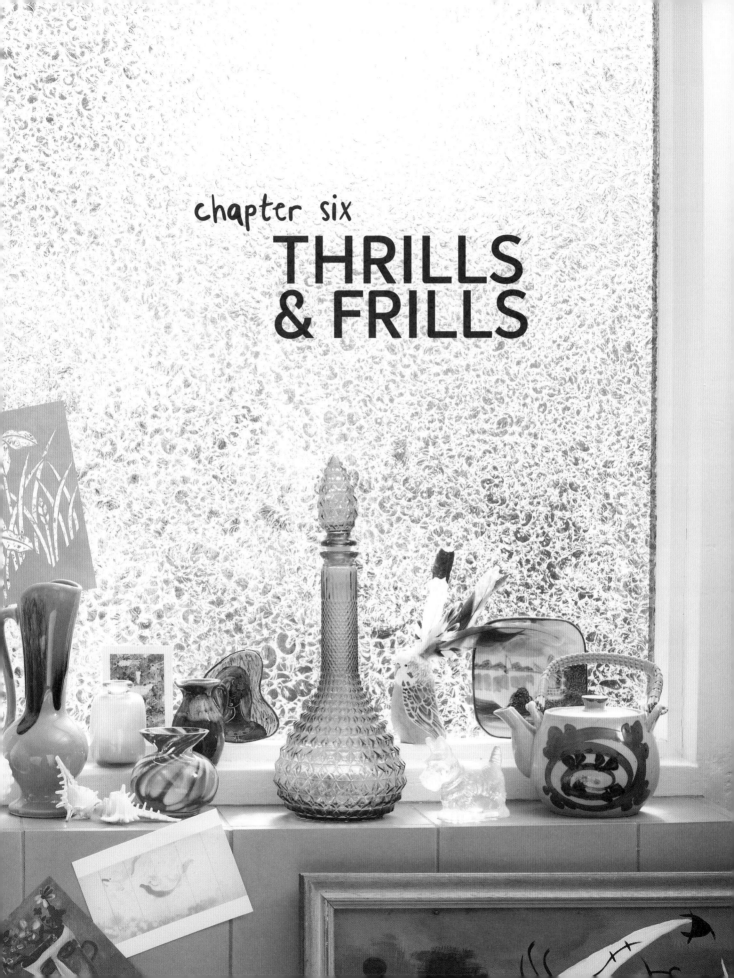

chapter six
THRILLS & FRILLS

Poached White Peaches with Orange Custard

We were in the tiniest village near Lake Orta in northern Italy, cooking dinner for some new friends. I had all the basics – fruit, wine, butter, eggs, flour, sugar, milk and cream – but no measuring equipment. After so many years of baking, I finally had that lightbulb moment, remembering I was armed with technique and, two hours later, I emerged proud, with silken poached peaches, a luscious pouring custard and puff pastry.

SERVES 4

INGREDIENTS
¼ quantity Rough Puff Pastry
  (see page 200)

POACHED PEACHES
125 ml (4 fl oz/½ cup) dry
  white wine
125 ml (4 fl oz/½ cup) water
110 g (3¾ oz/½ cup) sugar
1 teaspoon vanilla bean paste
  OR vanilla essence
2 white OR yellow peaches (not
  a clingstone variety)

ORANGE CUSTARD
250 ml (9 fl oz/1 cup) thickened
  (whipping) cream
250 ml (9 fl oz/1 cup) milk
1 teaspoon finely grated
  orange zest
4 egg yolks
40 g (1½ oz) caster (superfine)
  sugar
1 teaspoon vanilla extract OR
  vanilla essence

METHOD
Preheat the oven to 180°C (350°C) fan-forced. Have two identical baking trays on standby; line one with baking paper.

To bake the rough puff, on a lightly floured work surface, roll out the pastry into a 4 mm (³⁄₁₆ inch) thick rectangle. Place it on the lined tray, cover it with another sheet of baking paper, then pop the other tray on top. Bake for 30–40 minutes until a deep golden brown. Cool completely, before using a serrated knife to cut four pieces of puff in any shape you like. To cut the puff pastry, use a large sharp knife and cut in a sliding not pressing action, to avoid shattering the delicate layers of pastry. Place the puff in an airtight container, and set aside.

To poach the peaches, combine the wine, water, sugar and vanilla in a small saucepan over high heat. Bring to the boil, then lower in the peaches using a spoon. Cover and reduce to a simmer. Continue simmering for 5–10 minutes (depending on how big your peaches are) until the peaches are tender. Remove from the heat. When they are cool enough to handle, lift them out with a slotted spoon, then peel, halve and remove the stones. Chill the peach halves in the refrigerator until needed.

To make the orange custard, microwave the cream, milk and orange zest in a medium heatproof bowl for 3 minutes on the highest setting. In a medium mixing bowl, whisk the yolks, sugar and vanilla until pale and thick, then pour into the hot cream-and-milk mixture. Whisk well, then microwave in 90-second bursts, repeating this until the custard thickens enough to easily coat the back of a wooden spoon without running off immediately. See page 207 for tips on making a pouring custard. Chill before serving.

To serve, place a peach half in each bowl. Flood around the peaches with the custard, then garnish with a piece of puff.

Praline Custard Shortbreads

These are one of the most sensational biscuits I've ever tasted – almond shortbreads with a custard centre that oozes out the sides just enough for the amber jewels of almond praline to cling onto. Make sure you assemble these at the very last minute, or the praline will tragically start to dissolve from sitting against the moisture of the custard, and you will want to cry. However, you can bake the biscuits up to a week ahead of time.

MAKES ABOUT 24 BISCUITS

CUSTARD FILLING

250 ml (9 fl oz/1 cup) milk

3 egg yolks

50 g (1¾ oz) caster (superfine) sugar

1 teaspoon almond extract

25 g (1 oz) wheaten cornflour (cornstarch), see note on page 33

25 g (1 oz) chilled butter, cut into 1 cm (½ inch) cubes

ALMOND SHORTBREAD

150 g (5½ oz/1 cup) plain (all-purpose) flour

80 g (2¾ oz/¾ cup) almond meal

¼ teaspoon salt

2 tablespoons caster (superfine) sugar

90 g (3¼ oz) chilled unsalted butter, cut into 1 cm (½ inch) cubes

1 small egg

1 teaspoon almond OR vanilla extract

METHOD

To make the custard filling, microwave the milk in a heatproof bowl for 2 minutes on the highest setting. In a medium mixing bowl, whisk the yolks, sugar and almond extract until pale and thick. Add the cornflour, and whisk until smooth. Add the hot milk and whisk until combined, then microwave for another 2 minutes and whisk madly until smooth. The mixture should be a thick paste by now. Whisk in the butter, a few cubes at a time, until silky, then press plastic wrap directly onto the surface of the custard. Allow to cool completely to room temperature before using.

To make the shortbread, combine the flour, almond meal, salt and sugar in a food processor. Pulse for 2 seconds to mix the dry ingredients. Add the butter, and pulse until the mixture is a sandy consistency. Add the egg and almond extract, and pulse until the mixture begins to pull away from the side and gathers into a single mass. Tip the dough onto some plastic wrap, squash into a disc, wrap it up and rest in the refrigerator for 30 minutes before using.

Preheat the oven to 170°C (325°F) fan-forced. Line a baking tray with baking paper.

To bake the biscuits, roll out the dough on a lightly floured work surface until 3 mm (⅛ inch) thick, then cut out 5 cm (2 inch) circles with a pastry cutter. (If you re-roll the dough scraps, make sure you don't knead it – use a squeezing action so you don't activate the gluten and make the pastry tough. Also, rest it for another 20–30 minutes before re-rolling.) Place the circles of dough 2 cm (¾ inch) apart on the prepared tray. Bake for about 15 minutes until golden brown. Transfer the biscuits to wire racks, to cool completely before assembling.

To make the praline, spread the almonds in a single layer on some baking paper. Mix together the sugar and water in a small saucepan, then leave it alone to boil until you have a golden caramel. Make sure you do watch the caramel attentively while it cooks, as it will go from perfectly golden to smoking black in a second. As soon as it's near the colour you want, turn off the heat – the residual heat will cook the caramel further and turn it a deep amber. Immediately pour over the almonds, and allow it to set until completely hard. Break into small chunks, and pound lightly using a mortar and pestle until you have a fine crumb. If you pound too aggressively, you will compress the praline into a solid mass at the bottom of the mortar.

To assemble, sandwich pairs of biscuits with about a teaspoonful of the custard – enough so it oozes out ever so slightly – then dip the sticky sides into the praline crumble. Dust with icing sugar before serving.

PRALINE

35 g (1¼ oz/¼ cup) slivered almonds, toasted (see note on page 100)
75 g (2½ oz/⅓ cup) caster (superfine) sugar
2 tablespoons water

TO SERVE

Icing (confectioners') sugar, to dust

**MAGIC RAINBOW PIÑATA
BIRTHDAY CAKE**

Magic Rainbow Piñata Birthday Cake

This cake is the mother of all naughty birthday cakes. You should make it and not feel bad because whoever you make it for will think you are a god. It appeals to actual small children and metaphorical ones of the larger, taller kind. Either way, it's irresistibly fun, and you will feel like Willy Wonka when you wheel it out and everyone is filled with wonderment. Warning and disclaimer: definitely a sometimes food. Poh not responsible for any post-ingestion chaos that ensues from sugar high.

FEEDS UP TO 40

CAKE BATTER

1.125 kg (2 lb 12 oz/7½ cups) plain (all-purpose) flour, sifted

3 teaspoons bicarbonate of soda (baking soda), sifted

990 g (2 lb 3 oz/4½ cups) caster (superfine) sugar

1½ teaspoons salt

185 ml (6 fl oz/¾ cup) white vinegar

750ml (26 fl oz/3 cups) milk

3 teaspoons vanilla extract OR vanilla essence

600 g (1 lb 5 oz) unsalted butter, melted

6 eggs, lightly whisked

1–2 teaspoons each of 6 shades of food colouring (for the artistically challenged, mostly red with a little blue makes purple, mostly yellow with a little red makes orange, mostly yellow with a little blue makes green)

CREAM CHEESE FROSTING

750 g (1 lb 10 oz) cream cheese, softened

150 g (5½ oz) butter, softened

310 g (11 oz/2½ cups) icing (confectioners') sugar OR to taste

2 teaspoons vanilla extract

METHOD

Preheat the oven to 160°C (315°F) fan-forced. Grease and flour the sides of six identical 20 cm (8 inch) round cake tins. Line the bottom of each tin with baking paper.

To make the cake batter, combine the flour, bicarbonate of soda, sugar and salt in an extra large mixing bowl. Whisk briefly to mix and aerate the ingredients. In a jug, combine the vinegar, milk and vanilla. Add to the dry ingredients together with the melted butter and eggs. Whisk until the batter is combined.

Using a measuring cup, divide the batter *very* evenly among six medium mixing bowls. Whisk the food colouring into each bowl until you reach the intensity of tone you like, then transfer the different-coloured batters to the prepared tins – with a single colour in each tin.

Bake for 30 minutes, or until an inserted skewer in each cake comes out clean. Be careful you don't overcook the cakes, as the intensity of the food colouring fades when the cake browns more. If your oven is too small, you can bake three tins on a middle shelf, then when they come out bake the remaining three. Don't worry, this batter is very forgiving, and the ones waiting to be baked will not be affected. Carefully remove the cakes from their tins, and cool completely on wire racks before using.

To make the cream cheese frosting, combine the cream cheese, butter, icing sugar and vanilla in a large bowl, and beat with an electric mixer on high speed until smooth.

To prepare each layer of cake for stacking, carefully slice the domed part of each layer away, so you have a nice flat surface to work with. Stack the colours in the order you like, then set your selected top layer aside. Using an 8–9 cm (3¼–3½ inch) pastry cutter, carefully cut a circle at the centre of each remaining layer. Set the cut-out circles aside for later.

Begin to assemble the cake by placing the first layer on a serving plate or cake board. Spread a 5 mm (¼ inch) layer of the frosting between each layer, making sure you leave a 5 mm (¼ inch) border around the inner circle. Before you place the final layer (with no hole punched out of it) on top, pour your mixed chocolates or lollies into the hole. Spread a thin layer of cream cheese frosting over the entire surface of the cake. Place the iced cake in a large, clean cardboard box with 10 cm (4 inch) sides (and no holes) and gently cup the sprinkles against the edge so they stick to the frosting. Repeat this until the side of the cake is covered well.

To make the letters, slice each coloured cake circle in half horizontally. Using a small paring knife, carefully cut out the letters you need. Use a combination of toothpicks and bamboo skewers to give the letters stability and a variety of heights, but also to enable you to secure them to the cake (be careful that nobody accidentally eats one once you cut the cake!).

When cutting the cake, make sure a fair-sized wedge is cut and removed, to give the chocolates or lollies room to tumble out of the cake nicely. Good luck – I guarantee you'll have as much fun making this as the receiver will cutting it!

BITS & PIECES

About 3½ scant cups of small mixed chocolates OR lollies (sweets/candies) of choice

1½ scant cups of mixed sprinkles of choice

Strawberry Lychee Chiffon Cake

I made up this cake for one of Mum's birthdays – I wanted to make her something that was ultra girlie and instantly put a huge smile on her face. The perfume of this cake is gorgeously feminine – lychees and strawberries. With the spongiest, lightest of chiffons, little garden blooms and some pink cream to hold it all together, you have a pretty adorable cake. Best of all, no fancy-pants piping skills are required.

FEEDS 10–12

LYCHEE CHIFFON CAKE
5 eggs, separated + 2 extra
  egg whites
½ teaspoon cream of tartar
150 g (5½ oz/⅔ cup) caster
  (superfine) sugar
80 ml (2½ fl oz/⅓ cup) grapeseed
  oil OR vegetable oil
1 tablespoon Paraiso lychee liqueur
100 ml (3½ fl oz) tinned
  coconut milk
150 g (5½ oz/1 cup) plain
  (all-purpose) flour, sifted
2 teaspoons baking powder, sifted
Pinch of salt

BITS & PIECES
900 ml (30 fl oz/3½ cups)
  thickened (whipping) cream
90 g (3¼ oz/¾ cup) icing
  (confectioner's) sugar mixture
2 teaspoons Paraiso lychee liqueur
A few drops of red or pink food
  colouring
750 g (1 lb 10 oz) strawberries, tops
  removed, sliced lengthways
560 g (1 lb 4 oz) tinned pitted
  lychees, drained and
  roughly sliced
About 40 unsprayed snapdragons
  OR other edible flowers

METHOD
Preheat the oven to 170°C (325°F) fan-forced. Have a 25 cm (10 inch) angel food cake tin on standby. Do not grease or use a non-stick tin – for the chiffon to rise properly, sticky sides are exactly what the mixture needs to climb and sustain the impressive height.

To make the chiffon cake, first make a meringue. Combine the 7 egg whites and cream of tartar in a medium mixing bowl. Whisk with an electric mixer on high speed until medium peaks form. Add half the caster sugar, but only 1 tablespoon at a time, whisking well between each addition, until stiff peaks form. Set aside.

Next, combine the egg yolks and remaining sugar in a large mixing bowl, and whisk until pale and thick. Add the grapeseed oil, lychee liqueur and coconut milk, and whisk until combined. Add the flour, baking powder and salt, and whisk until just smooth.

Spoon one-third of the meringue mixture into the egg yolk mixture, and whisk until combined. Fold in the remaining meringue with a whisk, taking care to get rid of any small pockets of egg white.

Pour the mixture into the angel food cake tin, smooth out the surface and bake for 30–40 minutes, or until an inserted skewer comes out clean. Immediately invert the cake tin when it comes out of the oven, and cool completely before removing from the tin – this takes about 2 hours. Run a knife around the inner and outer sides of the tin, and you'll find the cooled cake will release easily. Next, slide the knife along the bottom of the tin, to free the cake completely.

To finish the cake, whisk the cream and icing sugar mixture until stiff peaks form. Add the lychee liqueur and food colouring, then whisk carefully by hand to combine.

Slice the cake horizontally into three layers. Spread two of the layers with the flavoured cream, evenly dotting the surface with strawberries and lychees, and stacking one on the other. Top with the third layer of cake, and thinly cover all over with the cream. Decorate as you wish with the remaining sliced strawberries and edible flowers.

Angel Food Cake

This is one of the most intriguing cakes I've ever made. The centre bakes bright white, then eating it is a slightly confusing affair because the texture is dense but also incredibly fluffy (a bit like a sponge crossed with a marshmallow pavlova). Don't go too hard trying to figure it out, though, or you'll wind up eating a good portion of a cake meant for twelve, like I did.

FEEDS 12–14

ANGEL FOOD CAKE

400 g (14 oz) egg whites OR
    12 large egg whites
1½ teaspoons cream of tartar
¼ teaspoon salt
220 g (7¾ oz/1 cup) caster
    (superfine) sugar
150 g (5½ oz/1 cup) plain
    (all-purpose) flour, sifted
1½ teaspoons vanilla extract OR
    vanilla essence

TO SERVE

1 quantity Crème Chantilly
    (see page 203) OR Yoghurt
    Mascarpone Cream (see
    page 206)
80 g (2¾ oz/¾ cup) toasted flaked
    almonds (see note on page 100)
250 g (9 oz/1⅔ cups) strawberries,
    halved or sliced

METHOD

Preheat the oven to 190°C (375°F) fan-forced. Have a 25 cm (10 inch) angel food cake tin on standby. Do not grease or use a non-stick tin – for the chiffon to rise properly, sticky sides are exactly what the mixture needs to climb and sustain the impressive height.

Combine the egg whites with the cream of tartar in a large bowl. Using an electric mixer, whisk on high speed until soft peaks form. Add the salt and then 1 tablespoon of the sugar at a time, whisking well between each addition, until all the sugar has been used and the meringue is glossy with stiff peaks.

Add the flour and vanilla, and fold gently with a whisk until combined. Pour the mixture into the angel food cake tin, and smooth out the surface. Reduce the oven temperature to 180°C (350°F) fan-forced, and bake for about 30 minutes, or until an inserted skewer comes out clean. Immediately invert the cake tin when it comes out of the oven, and allow the cake to cool completely before removing from the tin – about 2 hours.

To remove the cake from the tin, run a knife around the inner and outer sides of the tin, and you'll find that the cooled cake will release easily. Next, slide the knife along the bottom of the tin, to free the cake completely.

Serve with your choice of dolloping cream, a sprinkle of the almonds and a scattering of fresh strawberries.

Hummingbird Cake

The origins of this cake are actually Jamaican, where it's also known as the doctor bird cake. A cute Jamface customer once misread our sign and asked for a slice of 'humanbird cake', so this is what it's affectionately known as back of house. The thing that makes it ping a little more than your standard banana cake is the addition of crushed pineapple, coconut and pecans. It's wonderful as an indulgent tea cake, but also perfect for a special occasion.

FEEDS 12–16

INGREDIENTS

425 g (15 oz) tinned crushed
    pineapple in juice
450 g (1 lb/3 cups) plain
    (all-purpose) flour
1 teaspoon bicarbonate of soda
    (baking soda)
2 teaspoons baking powder
330 g (11½ oz/1½ cups firmly
    packed) soft brown sugar
1½ teaspoons ground cinnamon
⅛ teaspoon ground ginger
1 teaspoon salt
3 large eggs, lightly whisked
250 ml (9 fl oz/1 cup) vegetable oil
1½ teaspoons vanilla extract
    OR vanilla essence
4 medium bananas, chopped
35 g (1¼ oz/½ cup) dried shredded
    coconut
150 g (5½ oz) toasted pecans,
    roughly chopped (see first
    paragraph of Basic Nut Praline
    method on page 100)

CREAM CHEESE FROSTING

375 g (13 oz) cream cheese, softened
100 g (3½ oz) butter, softened
185 g (6½ oz/1½ cups) icing
    (confectioners') sugar
1 teaspoon vanilla extract
60 ml (2 fl oz/¼ cup) lemon juice

METHOD

Start by draining and squeezing the juice out of the pineapple. Pour the juice into a small saucepan and simmer over low heat until reduced by half. Set aside to cool.

Preheat the oven to 170°C (325°F) fan-forced. Grease and flour the sides of three 20 cm (8 inch) round cake tins. Line the bottoms with baking paper.

To make the cake batter, whisk the flour, bicarbonate of soda, baking powder, brown sugar, cinnamon, ginger and salt in a large mixing bowl, to combine and aerate. Add the eggs, vegetable oil, vanilla, bananas, pineapple, reduced pineapple juice, coconut and only 100 g (3½ oz) of the pecans, and stir gently until combined. Set the remaining pecans aside for decorating.

Make sure you spoon equal amounts of the mixture into each of the prepared tins, so the cakes cook evenly. Bake for about 30 minutes, or until an inserted skewer comes out clean. Turn out the cakes onto a wire rack to cool completely before icing.

To make the cream cheese frosting, combine the cream cheese and butter in the bowl of an electric stand mixer and, using the paddle attachment, beat until smooth. Add the icing sugar and vanilla and continue to beat until the sugar has dissolved and you have a lovely silky texture. Add the lemon juice, and stir with a whisk until combined.

Place the first layer of cake on your serving plate. Spread about 5 mm (¼ inch) of frosting on it, then repeat for the second layer. To finish, cover the entire cake with the frosting (but remember you don't have to use all of it), then sprinkle the reserved pecans on top.

Lemon Meringue Cloud Cake

One day, I was thinking how everyone loves a lemon meringue tart, and what if I were to transfer all those flavours and textures into the lightest of sponge cakes? It would be like eating a lemony cloud! And so this recipe was born. Please trust me when I suggest you buy a blowtorch from the local hardware store and not an expensive one from a fancy homewares shop.

FEEDS 12–14

SPONGE CAKE
6 eggs
165 g (5¾ oz / ¾ cup) caster (superfine) sugar
Pinch of salt
1 teaspoon grated lemon zest OR vanilla extract
100 g (3½ oz / ½ cup) plain (all-purpose) flour, sifted
60 g (2¼ oz / ¼ cup) wheaten cornflour (cornstarch), sifted (see note on page 33)
1½ teaspoons baking powder, sifted
60 g (2½ oz) butter, melted

LEMON CREAM
180 ml (6 fl oz / ¾ cup) thickened (whipping) cream
1 teaspoon finely grated lemon zest OR vanilla extract

BITS & PIECES
1 quantity Shannon's Lemon Curd (see page 208)
1 quantity Italian Meringue (see page 211)

METHOD
Preheat the oven to 170°C (325°F) fan-forced. Line the bottoms of two 20 cm (8 inch) round cake tins with baking paper; grease and flour the sides.

To make the sponge, combine the eggs, sugar, salt and lemon zest in a medium mixing bowl, and whisk with an electric mixer on high speed until the mixture triples in volume and is very pale and fluffy. Add the flour, cornflour and baking powder in three batches, folding very gently with a whisk and making sure no pockets of flour remain, especially at the bottom of the bowl. Add the butter, and fold carefully to combine.

Pour into the prepared tins, and bake for about 25 minutes, or until an inserted skewer comes out clean. When the sponges come out of the oven, run a paring knife around the edge of the tins to release the sides. Turn out onto a wire rack and cool completely before assembling.

Meanwhile, to make the lemon cream, combine the cream and lemon zest in a medium mixing bowl, and whisk until stiff peaks form. Chill until needed.

To assemble the cake, slice each cake in half horizontally. Place the first layer on a serving plate, and spread half the lemon curd to cover the surface. Pop the second layer on top and cover with the lemon cream. Over this, place the third layer of sponge, followed by the remaining lemon curd and then the final tier of cake.

To 'ice' the cake, first spread the thinnest possible layer of the meringue over the entire cake, so you have a nice white base to work with. This way, any little gaps you might leave between the piping won't show up as little brown dots. Transfer the remaining meringue to a piping bag fitted with a round or star nozzle (large or small is up to you), then systematically pipe 'kisses' of meringue to cover the cake.

Now, the fun part. Using a blowtorch, torch all the tips of meringue; I love mine a bit scorched because slightly burnt meringue is *the* best but, if you prefer it golden and dainty instead, go ahead!

Banana Cinnamon Date Stacks

A chewy, cinnamony dacquoise base studded with sticky dates, layered with fresh cream, sliced banana and toasted almonds, then finished with lashings of dark chocolate ganache – what's not to like?

MAKES ABOUT 10 STACKS

DACQUOISE

6 large egg whites
300 g (10½ oz/1⅓ cups) caster (superfine) sugar
150 g (5½ oz/1½ cups) almond meal, sifted
1½ teaspoons ground cinnamon
100 g (3½ oz) pitted dates, roughly chopped

GANACHE

80 ml (2½ fl oz/⅓ cup) thickened (whipping) cream
100 g (3½ oz/⅔ cup) dark chocolate melts (buttons) OR chopped dark chocolate

BITS & PIECES

2 quantities Crème Chantilly (see page 203)
6 bananas
160 g (5¾ oz/1 cup) toasted almonds, roughly chopped (see first paragraph of Basic Nut Praline method on page 100)

METHOD

Preheat the oven to 130°C (250°F) fan-forced. Line four baking trays with baking paper. Draw a total of twenty 8 cm (3¼ inch) circles on the baking paper, leaving at least 3 cm (1¼ inches) space between them. Spread these out over the baking trays.

To make the dacquoise bases, in a large bowl, whisk the egg whites with an electric mixer on high speed until medium peaks form. Start adding a tablespoonful of the sugar at a time, whisking well between each addition. Keep whisking until all the sugar has been used and the meringue is very stiff and glossy. Combine the almond meal and cinnamon in a small bowl, and mix briefly. Add this, together with the dates, to the meringue, and fold together to combine.

Transfer the mixture to a piping bag, and snip a 1 cm (½ inch) hole off the tip. Pipe concentric circles onto the prepared baking paper, or simply use a spoon or spatula to spread the mixture. Bake for 30 minutes. Cool completely on the trays before using.

To make the ganache, microwave the cream and chocolate in a small heatproof bowl for about 40 seconds on the highest setting. Whisk until smooth, then transfer the ganache to a piping bag.

To assemble the stacks, just before serving, spread a dollop of the Crème Chantilly on a disc of dacquoise. Slice the bananas and arrange a layer of them on the cream, then snip a 2 mm (1/16 inch) hole off the tip of the piping bag holding the ganache. Squeeze a zigzag of ganache over the top of the bananas, then finish with a sprinkle of almonds. Place another disc of dacquoise on top, and repeat the process. Continue until all the stacks are made, or assemble them as you need – the dacquoise discs will last up to a week in an airtight container. Serve immediately after assembling.

Flourless Chocolate Cake with Guinness Ice Cream

If you want to rock up at a party feeling like a total legend, then bring this ... because everyone knows that chocolate + beer = happiness. In cake and ice cream form, double happiness.

FEEDS UP TO 12

ICE CREAM OR PARFAIT
560 ml (19¼ fl oz/2¼ cups) Guinness, dark ale OR stout
560 ml (19¼ fl oz/2¼ cups) thickened (whipping) cream
180 g (6½ oz) caster (superfine) sugar
12 egg yolks

FLOURLESS CHOCOLATE CAKE
250 g (9 oz) unsalted butter
300 g (10½ oz/1⅓ cups firmly packed) soft dark brown sugar
80 ml (2½ fl oz/⅓ cup) water
250 g (9 oz/1⅔ cups) dark chocolate melts (buttons) OR chopped dark chocolate (75% cocoa solids)
6 eggs, separated
30 ml (1 fl oz) brandy
¼ teaspoon salt
Dutch process cocoa powder, to dust

TO SERVE
Fresh raspberries, to garnish (optional)

METHOD

To make the ice cream, microwave the Guinness and cream in a heatproof bowl for 4 minutes on the highest setting.

Combine the caster sugar and egg yolks in a medium mixing bowl, and whisk until pale and thick. Add to the hot Guinness-and-cream mixture, and whisk to combine – see notes.

Microwave for 1½ minutes on the highest setting, then whisk briskly. Continue to microwave in 1-minute bursts, whisking well in between, until the mixture is thick enough to easily coat the back of a wooden spoon. Be careful not to overcook it, or it will split and look a little dotty – see notes.

Chill the custard completely, before churning in an ice-cream machine following the manufacturer's instructions. If you don't own one, make a parfait (unchurned ice cream) instead by pouring the custard into a container lined with baking paper or foil – make sure there is about 4 cm (1½ inches) of overhang. Cover and freeze completely before using.

Preheat the oven to 180°C (350°F) fan-forced. Grease the ring of a 24 cm (9½ inch) springform tin, then turn the base upside down, so it no longer has a lip. Place a piece of baking paper over it, then clamp the ring around it to secure.

To make the chocolate cake, combine the butter, brown sugar and water in a medium saucepan over medium heat. Stir until the sugar has dissolved, then remove from the heat and whisk in the chocolate. Add the egg yolks, brandy and salt, and whisk until combined.

Next, in a large mixing bowl (make sure it's completely clean and dry), whisk the egg whites using an electric mixer on the highest speed until they just begin to form stiff peaks and no more. Whisk one-third of the egg whites into the chocolate cake batter to loosen the mixture a little. Add the remainder, and stir gently with the whisk to combine. Pour the batter into the prepared tin, and bake for about 20 minutes. You want the centre to be just done and have a slight wobble, but not be undercooked. Remove from the oven, set on a wire rack and allow the cake to cool completely in the tin – about 1 hour. Don't be worried if the cake collapses a little in the middle after cooling.

Transfer to a serving plate, dust well with cocoa and cut into 10 or 12 slices. Serve each slice with a scoop of Guinness ice cream, and garnish with 3 or 4 fresh raspberries per serving. If you made a parfait, use the overhanging baking paper or foil to lift it out of its container and slice to serve.

NOTES

Whenever you are combining sugar and eggs in a bowl, never allow the sugar to rest on the eggs for any length of time before whisking vigorously or it will pickle the yolks unevenly and create a lumpy texture.

If you ever split a custard mixture, immediately blitz with a blender or stick blender. This will hopefully restore it to a smooth mixture again. If not, you'll have to start from scratch again, I'm afraid.

FLOURLESS CHOCOLATE CAKE
WITH GUINNESS ICE CREAM

Jaffa Lamington Chiffon Cake

Mr Lamington, meet Miss Orange Chiffon – fluffy, chocolatey, jaffy, coconutty goodness ... and they lived happily ever after.

FEEDS 10–12

ORANGE CHIFFON CAKE

5 eggs, separated + 2 extra
    egg whites
½ teaspoon cream of tartar
150 g (5½ oz/⅔ cup) caster
    (superfine) sugar
80 ml (2½ fl oz/⅓ cup) grapeseed
    oil OR vegetable oil
Finely grated zest of 1 orange
80 ml (2½ fl oz/⅓ cup) orange juice
100 ml (3½ fl oz) tinned
    coconut milk
150 g (5½ oz) plain (all-purpose)
    flour, sifted
2 teaspoons baking powder, sifted
Pinch of salt

CHOCOLATE ICING

290 g (10¼ oz) icing (confectioners')
    sugar mixture
28 g (1 oz) Dutch process cocoa
    powder
20 g (¾ oz) butter
90 ml (3 fl oz) milk

TO DECORATE

125 g (4½ oz/about 1⅓ cups) dried
    shredded OR desiccated coconut

METHOD

Preheat the oven to 170°C (325°F) fan-forced. Have a 25 cm (10 inch) angel food cake tin on standby. Do not grease or use a non-stick tin – for the chiffon to rise properly, sticky sides are exactly what the mixture needs to climb and sustain the impressive height.

To make the orange chiffon cake, first make a meringue. Combine the 7 egg whites and cream of tartar in a medium mixing bowl. Whisk with an electric mixer on high speed until medium peaks form. Add half the caster sugar 1 tablespoon at a time, whisking well between each addition until stiff peaks form. Set aside.

In a large bowl, whisk the egg yolks and remaining sugar until pale and thick. Add the grapeseed oil, orange zest and juice, and coconut milk, and whisk until combined. Add the flour, baking powder and salt, and whisk until just smooth.

Spoon one-third of the meringue mixture into the egg yolk mixture, and whisk until combined. Fold in the remaining meringue with a whisk, taking care to get rid of any small pockets of egg white.

Pour the mixture into the angel food cake tin, smooth out the surface and bake for 30–40 minutes, or until an inserted skewer comes out clean. Immediately invert the cake tin when it comes out of the oven, and allow the cake to cool completely before removing from the tin – about 2 hours. Run a knife around the inner and outer sides of the tin, and you'll find that the cooled cake will release easily. Next, slide the knife along the bottom of the tin, to free the cake completely.

To make the chocolate icing, combine the icing sugar, cocoa, butter and milk in a heatproof bowl. Sit it over a saucepan filled with 4 cm (1½ inches) simmering water, and whisk until the icing sugar has dissolved. Using a spatula, spread the runny chocolate mixture over the entire cake, then cover with the coconut. This cake will keep well for 3–4 days if stored in an airtight container.

TIP

If the icing starts to seize up, microwave for about 10 seconds, then stir to loosen the mixture.

Hazelnut & Lime Tutus

I'm notorious for whining my head off about cupcakes because they're usually little clumps of bad-quality cake tizzied up in frothy outfits, so the mission was to design one with looks *and* personality. The 'inspo' combo comes from one of my favourite cocktails – lime and Frangelico liqueur – then I kept adding layers and things got serious …

MAKES 12 CUPCAKES

CUPCAKE BATTER

100 g (3½ oz) unsalted butter, softened
185 g (6½ oz) caster (superfine) sugar
1 teaspoon vanilla extract
2 large eggs
125 ml (4 fl oz/½ cup) milk
80 g (2¾ oz/¾ cup) hazelnut meal, sifted
120 g (4¼ oz) plain (all-purpose) flour, sifted
1½ teaspoons baking powder, sifted

STEWED APPLES

180 g (6 oz) pink lady OR granny smith apples
Pinch of ground cinnamon
2 teaspoons soft brown sugar
100 ml (3½ fl oz) apple juice
45 ml (1½ fl oz) Frangelico liqueur
Finely grated zest of 1 lime

CANDIED LIME ZEST

Zest of 1 lime (use an old-fashioned zester that makes spirals)
250 ml (9 fl oz/1 cup) boiling water
3 tablespoons caster (superfine) sugar
1 tablespoon water

TO FINISH

1 quantity Crème Chantilly, whisked to stiff peaks (see page 203)

METHOD

Preheat the oven to 170°C (325°) fan-forced. Grease and flour a standard 12-hole muffin tin.

To make the cupcake batter, combine the butter, sugar and vanilla in a medium mixing bowl, and beat with an electric mixer on high speed until pale and fluffy. Add the eggs and milk, and beat until combined. Using a rubber spatula, fold in the hazelnut meal, flour and baking powder. Fill each of the muffin holes until three-quarters full of batter, and bake for 15–20 minutes, or until golden and an inserted skewer comes out clean. Turn the muffin tin upside down to release the cupcakes as soon as they come out of the oven. Transfer to a wire rack, right way up, to cool completely before filling.

To stew the apples, peel, core and quarter them, then cut into slices 3 mm (⅛ inch) thick. Combine them with the cinnamon, sugar, apple juice, Frangelico liqueur and lime zest in a small saucepan. Cook, covered, over medium heat until most of the liquid has evaporated. The apples will be soft but should still hold their shape, and have a residual crunch. Spread the apple out on a plate to cool, then chill until ready to use.

To make the candied lime zest, first place the zest in a small bowl, then cover with the boiling water. Drain the zest in a sieve, then combine it with the sugar and the 1 tablespoon water in a small saucepan. Simmer until most of the water has evaporated and the zest is very sticky. Set aside to cool.

To assemble your 'tutus', transfer the Crème Chantilly to a piping bag fitted with a 1 cm (½ inch) star nozzle. Fan 12 x three layers of paper cases progressively flatter, to emulate a tutu. Slice each cupcake into three horizontal layers. Place a bottom layer of each of the cupcakes on a prepared 'tutu'. Pipe a small amount of the Crème Chantilly on the bottom layer, then arrange a layer of apple on top. Repeat for the second layer. To finish, put the top layer on each cupcake. Pipe rosettes of the Crème Chantilly to cover the top layer, then finish with the candied lime zest. Serve immediately.

Apple Caramel Cheesecake

I cannot wax lyrical enough about this cheesecake. We know apples and cheese have gone together for ever. Add caramel and Calvados, and you have a super-indulgent, classy cheesecake that makes people lose their minds, it's so delicious.

FEEDS 12–14

CRUMB BASE

180 g (6 oz) digestive biscuits (graham crackers)

150 g (5½ oz) toasted pecans (see first paragraph of Basic Nut Praline method on page 100), reserve 25 g (1 oz/¼ cup) to garnish

1 tablespoon soft brown sugar

100 g (3½ oz) unsalted butter, melted

¼ teaspoon salt

FILLING

750 g (1 lb 10 oz) cream cheese, softened

75 g (2½ oz/⅓ cup) caster (superfine) sugar

110 g (3¾ oz/½ cup firmly packed) soft brown sugar

1 teaspoon vanilla bean paste OR vanilla extract

2 teaspoons finely grated orange zest

4 large eggs

125 ml (4 fl oz/½ cup) thickened (whipping) cream

3 tablespoons lemon juice

METHOD

Preheat the oven to 160°C (315°F) fan-forced. Grease the ring of a 24 cm (9½ inch) springform tin, then turn the base upside down, so it no longer has a lip. Place a piece of baking paper over the base, then clamp the ring around it to secure.

To make the crumb base, combine the biscuits, pecans and brown sugar in a food processor, and pulse until you have a fine sandy texture. Add the butter and salt, and pulse until the mixture begins to pull together. Spread the crumb mixture evenly over the bottom of the prepared tin. Using a rubber spatula or your hands, press firmly into the base.

To make the filling, combine the cream cheese, sugars, vanilla and orange zest in a medium mixing bowl, and whisk with an electric mixer on high speed until light and fluffy. Add the eggs one at a time, whisking well between each addition. Add the cream, and whisk until just combined. Next, add the lemon juice and whisk by hand until just combined. Pour the mixture into the prepared tin, and bake for 40–50 minutes until the filling is just set and still a little wobbly.

Turn off the oven, prop the door ajar with a wooden spoon and allow the cheesecake to cool gradually for 1 hour. Leave the cheesecake in the tin, place it on a wire rack and cool completely – about 2 hours. Cover with a plate, and refrigerate for at least 4 hours or preferably overnight until chilled through.

To make the apple topping, combine the apple juice and vanilla in a medium saucepan, and bring to the boil. Reduce to a simmer, and cook until slightly thickened and reduced to 125 ml (4 fl oz/½ cup) in volume. Stir in the butter until melted. Add the apple slices and cook, stirring occasionally, until wilted. Add the brandy, and continue cooking until there is just enough syrup to coat the apples.

To make the caramel sauce, in a medium saucepan, stir the sugar and water with a metal spoon to combine, then bring to the boil. Continue boiling until the mixture turns a beautiful deep amber, then immediately remove from the heat. Slowly pour in a small amount of the cream – the mixture will bubble up aggressively, so be careful. Pour in the remaining cream, add the salt and whisk quickly to combine. Mix in the brandy and vanilla.

To serve, run a small paring knife around the edge of the tin, release the ring, then carefully slide the cheesecake onto a serving plate. Arrange the apple topping however you like. Drizzle with the caramel sauce, and sprinkle with the reserved toasted pecans. Serve additional sauce on the side.

APPLE TOPPING

250 ml (9 fl oz/1 cup) apple juice

1 teaspoon vanilla bean paste
  OR vanilla extract

20 g (¾ oz) butter

4 pink lady OR granny smith apples, peeled, cored and cut into 2 mm (¹⁄₁₆ inch) slices

60 ml (2 fl oz/¼ cup) brandy (preferably Calvados)

CARAMEL SAUCE

75 g (2½ oz/⅓ cup) caster (superfine) sugar

2 tablespoons water

100 ml (3½ fl oz) thickened (whipping) cream

¼ teaspoon salt

1 tablespoon brandy (preferably Calvados)

½ teaspoon vanilla extract
  OR vanilla essence

APPLE CARAMEL
CHEESECAKE

FLOURLESS VENETIAN CARROT CAKE

Flourless Venetian Carrot Cake

I couldn't handle breaking the marriage of carrot cake and cream cheese, so I didn't. With a bit of help from some white balsamic, this stays true to the Italian interpretation of the classic we know and love. White chocolate ganache is then lavished on a rich, moist olive oil-based cake punctuated with creamy pine nuts and rum-soaked sultanas ... Are you convinced yet? If you can't be bothered fussing with the baby bundt tins, follow the same instructions, but use a lined 20 cm (8 inch) round cake tin instead, and bake for about 40 minutes. When it's time to assemble, I'd sandwich two layers of the cake with not too much cream cheese, then cover it with the white chocky ganache.

MAKES 18 SMALL CAKES

INGREDIENTS

85 g (3 oz/½ cup) sultanas (golden raisins)
60 ml (2 fl oz/¼ cup) rum
3 eggs
165 g (5¾ oz/¾ cup) caster (superfine) sugar
1 teaspoon vanilla extract OR vanilla essence
125 ml (4 fl oz/½ cup) olive oil
2 carrots, grated
250 g (9 oz/2½ cups) almond meal
Finely grated zest of ½ lemon OR orange
1 tablespoon lemon juice
⅛ teaspoon freshly ground or grated nutmeg

WHITE CHOCOLATE GANACHE

50 g (1¾ oz) thin (pouring) cream
100 g (3½ oz/⅔ cup) white chocolate melts (buttons) OR finely chopped white chocolate
40 g (1½ oz/¼ cup) pine nuts, toasted (see first paragraph of Basic Nut Praline method on page 100)

METHOD

Preheat the oven to 160°C (315°F) fan-forced. Grease 18 baby bundt tins well with melted butter.

To prepare the sultanas, bring the sultanas and rum to the boil in a small saucepan. Reduce the heat, and simmer until the sultanas are plumped up and barely any liquid is left. Cool completely before using.

To make the cake, in a medium mixing bowl, whisk the eggs, sugar and vanilla with an electric mixer on high speed until pale and thick. Slowly drizzle in the olive oil, and continue to whisk until combined. Don't worry when the mixture drops in volume at this stage. Add the carrots, almond meal, lemon zest and juice, nutmeg and rum-soaked sultanas. Fold until the ingredients are just combined.

Spoon carefully into the prepared bundt tins, leaving 1 cm (½ inch) space at the top for the cakes to expand into. Bake for about 20 minutes, or until golden and an inserted skewer comes out clean. Rest in the tin for only a few seconds, before turning out the cakes onto a wire rack to cool completely.

To make the white chocolate ganache, microwave the cream and white chocolate in a small heatproof bowl for 1 minute on the highest setting, then whisk until smooth. Allow the ganache to cool a little, then transfer to a piping bag with a 2–3 mm (1/16 – 1/18 inch) hole snipped off the tip.

Place the individual cakes onto cake boards or a serving dish, and carefully drizzle the ganache attractively over each cake. Drop a few pine nuts on top before the ganache sets.

To make the cream cheese frosting, combine the cream cheese and butter in a medium mixing bowl, and beat with an electric mixer on high speed until combined. Add the icing sugar, and whisk until light and fluffy. Add the zest and balsamic vinegar, and stir vigorously with a wooden spoon until completely combined.

Transfer the frosting to a piping bag fitted with a small star nozzle, and pipe a border of stars around the base of each cake. Frosted or unfrosted, these cakes keep well for up to a week if stored in an airtight container.

WHITE BALSAMIC CREAM CHEESE FROSTING

250 g (9 oz) cream cheese, softened

50 g (1¾ oz) unsalted butter, softened

90 g (3¼ oz/¾ cup) icing (confectioners') sugar

Finely grated zest of ½ lemon OR orange

1½ tablespoons white balsamic vinegar

Rosewater Pistachio Meringues

We whip up a *lot* of custards at Jamface, and the tons of surplus egg whites are the reason we started making these. One thing I've discovered is that meringues have a magical way of making adults go all cute and gleeful. Ours are on the larger side, but you can pipe delicate little rosettes or domes instead. However, you'll need to alter the cooking time, which might take some experimenting. Just ensure any vessels and utensils you use are squeaky clean – the tiniest bit of oil, moisture or egg yolk will interfere with the meringue whipping up properly.

MAKES ABOUT 10 LARGE MERINGUES

INGREDIENTS
250 g (9 oz) egg whites
500 g (1 lb 2 oz) caster (superfine)
  sugar
½–1 teaspoon rosewater
Pink food colouring
2–3 tablespoons finely chopped
  pistachio nut kernels

METHOD
Preheat the oven to 130°C (250°F) fan-forced. Line two baking trays with baking paper.

To make the meringues, whisk the egg whites and sugar in a large heatproof bowl until combined. Sit the bowl over a large saucepan filled one-third with simmering water, and stir with a whisk until the sugar has completely dissolved – you'll find the mixture turns clear when this happens. If you aren't sure, rub the mixture between your fingers, to detect any undissolved grains.

Transfer the mixture to an electric stand mixer with a whisk attachment, and whisk on high speed until the mixture has cooled completely – about 10 minutes. You can gauge this by just touching the outside of the mixing bowl. Fold in the rosewater and enough food colouring to stain the meringue a pale pink until combined.

Spoon tennis ball–sized amounts of meringue onto the prepared baking trays, and sprinkle with the pistachios. Reduce the oven temperature to 100°C (200°F) fan-forced, and bake for 1½ hours. You'll end up with a crunchy outer shell, but the inside of the meringues will be soft and marshmallowy.

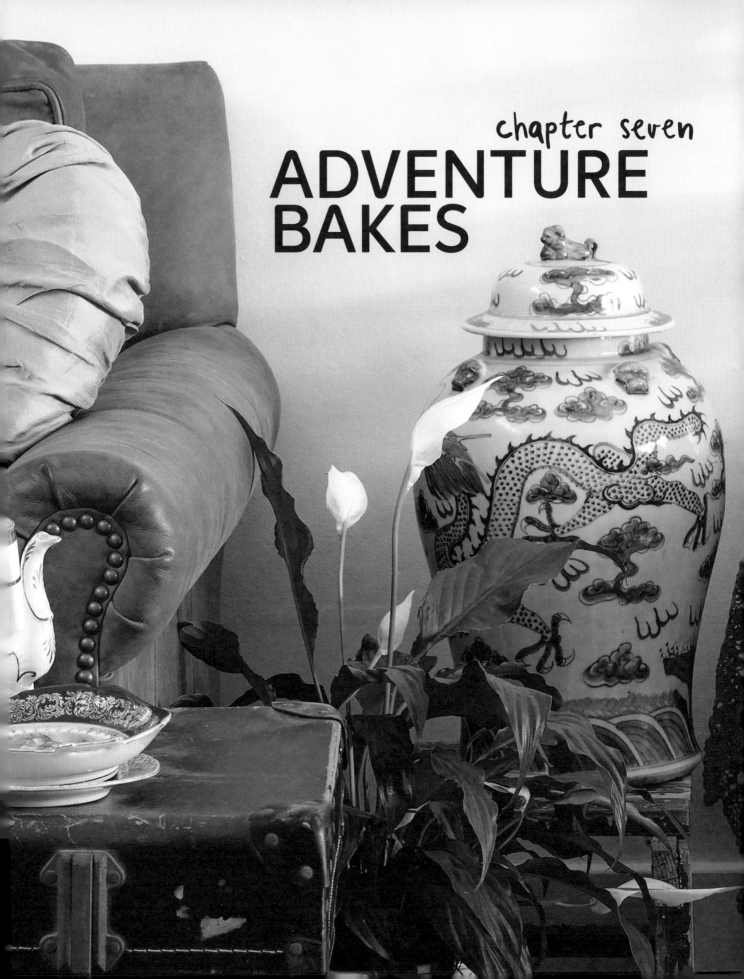

chapter seven
ADVENTURE
BAKES

Rotweinkuchen – German Red Wine Cake

This is a great recipe to make with a few drops of leftover wine – a moist tea cake with echoes of Christmas in the cinnamon, dark chocky and red wine. It has a puddingy kind of texture, so some fresh raspberries or blackberries with a bit of brandy or rum custard (see page 207) to pour over it on a winter's night would not go astray.

FEEDS 12–14

INGREDIENTS

4 eggs, separated
250 g (9 oz) unsalted butter, softened
250 g (9 oz) caster (superfine) sugar
¼ teaspoon salt
1 teaspoon vanilla extract OR vanilla essence
250 g (9 oz/1⅔ cups) plain (all-purpose) flour, sifted
1 teaspoon baking powder, sifted
2 teaspoons ground cinnamon
100 g (3½ oz/⅔ cup) dark chocolate melts (buttons) OR chopped dark chocolate
125 ml (4 fl oz/½ cup) red wine

TO SERVE

1 quantity Rum Custard (see page 207) OR Crème Chantilly (see page 203)

METHOD

Preheat the oven to 170°C (325°F) fan-forced. Grease and flour a 25 cm (10 inch) bundt tin.

So you don't have to clean your beaters in between, whisk the egg whites first, in a medium mixing bowl with an electric mixer on high speed, until medium peaks form. Set aside.

Combine the butter, sugar, salt and vanilla in a separate medium mixing bowl, and beat with an electric mixer on high speed until pale and fluffy. Add the egg yolks one at a time, beating well between each addition. Next, add the flour, baking powder, cinnamon and chocolate, and fold until combined. Pour in the wine, and stir with a whisk until combined. Whisk in one-third of the egg whites, to loosen the mixture, then add the remaining whites and stir gently with a whisk until combined. Pour the mixture into the prepared tin.

Bake for 40–50 minutes, or until an inserted skewer comes out clean. Turn out the cake immediately (or it will stick) onto a wire rack, and allow to cool. Serve with warm Rum Custard or Crème Chantilly.

Baumkuchen – German Tree Cake

Apart from being absolutely delicious, this to me is one of the most intriguing cakes ever invented. Traditionally, thin layers of batter are brushed onto a rotisserie, creating an effect that resembles the rings of a tree trunk. It fascinates me mostly because I grew up eating the Indonesian version of this grilled, not baked, layer cake. Its true origins are unknown, except that this method of making cakes was already practised in Ancient Greece, and it is speculated that the Germans inherited it from their Roman conquerors. If only recipes could talk …

FEEDS 16

CAKE BATTER

10 eggs, separated

Pinch of salt

90 g (3¼ oz / ¾ cup) icing (confectioners') sugar

280 g (10 oz) unsalted butter, softened

250 g (9 oz) marzipan, coarsely grated

1 teaspoon vanilla extract OR vanilla essence

Finely grated zest of 1 orange OR lemon

⅛ teaspoon salt

2 tablespoons dark rum

100 ml (3½ fl oz) thin (pouring) OR thickened (whipping) cream

125 g (4½ oz) plain (all-purpose) flour, sifted

½ teaspoon baking powder, sifted

METHOD

Grease and flour the side of a 23–25 cm (9–10 inch) round cake tin, then line the bottom with baking paper.

Place the egg whites in a large bowl with a pinch of salt, and whisk with an electric mixer on high speed until soft peaks form. Add only half the icing sugar, but 1 tablespoon at a time. Whisk well between each addition, until stiff peaks form. Set aside.

Combine the butter, marzipan, remaining sugar, vanilla, zest and salt in the bowl of an electric stand mixer. Using the paddle attachment, beat on high speed until pale and fluffy. Add the egg yolks one at a time, beating well between each addition. Whisk in the rum and cream, then fold in the flour and baking powder. Whisk in one-third of the egg whites to loosen the mixture. Add the remainder, and stir gently with a whisk until combined.

Preheat the oven grill (broiler) for 2 minutes on medium, then spread 125 ml (4 fl oz / ½ cup) of the cake batter very evenly over the bottom of the tin. Grill until cooked through and evenly golden brown (2–4 minutes). Repeat this process until all the batter has been used up. Keep in mind that, as the cake gets higher, the surface will brown more quickly but might not cook through, so you might have to place the tin on a lower shelf about three-quarters of the way through.

Allow the cake to cool for 2 minutes, before running a paring knife around the edge of the tin to release the side. Turn out the cake onto

>> **continued overleaf**

>> **from previous page**

BITS & PIECES

165 g (5¾ oz/½ cup) apricot jam
    OR marmalade, mixed with
    1 tablespoon hot water
1 quantity Dark Chocolate Ganache
    (see page 202)
25 g (1 oz/¼ cup) roasted flaked
    almonds (optional) (see note on
    page 100)

TO SERVE

1 quantity Crème Chantilly OR
    Vanilla Crème Fraîche (for both,
    see page 203)

a wire rack, and, while hot, baste all over with the jam. If the jam's very thick, water down further with a little more hot water. Allow to cool completely before icing.

To ice the cake, place it on a serving plate. Tuck strips of baking paper under the cake to catch any falling ganache and keep your plate clean. Pour the ganache over the cake, and spread to cover the entire surface. Keep catching any cascading chocolate with a small rubber spatula and scooping it back onto the top of the cake until the ganache sets. Don't overwork the ganache, or it will lose its gloss and become dull and matte. Carefully remove the strips of baking paper before sprinkling the flaked almonds over the top. Serve with your choice of dolloping cream.

Black Forest Crepe Cake

I'm not sure if it's that I was at too many birthdays as a kid where bad versions were served up or that it seemed to be the default cake of the 1970s and 1980s, but I've not had a black forest cake for decades. It's been long enough, so I thought I'd revisit the idea in crepe form because crepes are my absolute favourite.

FEEDS 15–20

CHOCOLATE CREPE BATTER

110 g (3¾ oz/ ¾ cup) plain (all-purpose) flour, sifted
4 large eggs
¼ teaspoon salt
2 tablespoons caster (superfine) sugar
2 tablespoons Dutch process cocoa powder
1 teaspoon vanilla extract OR vanilla essence
2 tablespoons melted butter OR vegetable oil
500 ml (17 fl oz/2 cups) milk

BITS & PIECES

700 g (1 lb 9 oz) morello cherries in light syrup, drained
2 tablespoons kirsch OR Frangelico liqueur
2 tablespoons icing (confectioners') sugar
1½ quantities Dark OR Milk Chocolate Ganache (see page 202)
2 quantities Crème Chantilly OR Vanilla Crème Fraîche (for both, see page 203) OR Yoghurt Mascarpone Cream (see page 206)

METHOD

To make the chocolate crepes, whisk the flour, eggs, salt, caster sugar, cocoa, vanilla, melted butter and one-third of the milk in a medium mixing bowl until smooth. Add the remainder of the milk, and stir until combined – the batter should be quite runny. If something went wrong and you have a lumpy mess, pass the batter through a sieve.

Grease a 20–22 cm (8–8¼ inch) non-stick frying pan, and place over medium heat for about 2 minutes. Pour in 60–80 ml (2–2½ fl oz/ ¼–⅓ cup) of the crepe batter, and work quickly to roll it around to cover the bottom of the pan completely. If the pan isn't hot enough, the batter will slide around and not stick. Get it hotter, and try again.

When the edges of the crepe become a bit papery and dry, they will pull away from the frying pan. Using a spatula or butter knife, pry an edge away and, using just the tips of your fingers, flip the crepe upside down and cook for mere seconds before transferring to a plate. Repeat until all the batter has been used, resting the crepes that are still warm on a wire rack; you will end up with about 15 crepes. Cool completely, before piling them on top of one another.

To prepare the morello cherries, combine them with the kirsch and icing sugar in a small bowl. Stir to combine, and refrigerate until needed. Transfer the ganache to a piping bag with a 2 mm (¹⁄₁₆ inch) hole snipped off the tip.

To assemble the cake, place a crepe on your serving plate, and spread with the thinnest possible layer of Crème Chantilly to cover it. Squeeze a thin zigzag of the ganache across the surface. Repeat this process until you have used all your crepes. You can choose to space out the cherries over each layer, but you have to divide them among the number of crepe layers you have first, so you don't run out. Otherwise, spread them more densely across three layers, one close to the bottom, one in the middle and one close to the top.

To finish, take any remaining ganache and swirl over the top of the cake.

Portuguese Custard Tarts

There are two significant things that make these no ordinary custard tarts. One is the use of puff pastry instead of a shortcrust, the other is that this is not just regular puff, but puff that's layered with cinnamon. The pastry is then rolled into a cylinder, cut into discs and pushed into the moulds so that the layers bake radiating outwards like the rings of a tree. For a different nuance, you can use ground cardamom instead of cinnamon.

MAKES 16 INDIVIDUAL TARTS

INGREDIENTS

1 quantity Rough Puff Pastry (see page 200)
1–2 teaspoons ground cinnamon OR ground cardamom + extra, to sprinkle

CUSTARD

600 ml (21 fl oz) milk
2 eggs + 2 extra yolks
2 teaspoons vanilla extract OR vanilla essence
170 g (6 oz/¾ cup) caster (superfine) sugar
2½ tablespoons wheaten cornflour (cornstarch), see note on page 33

METHOD

To make the custard, microwave the milk in a heatproof bowl for 3 minutes on the highest setting. In another medium mixing bowl, whisk the eggs, extra yolks, vanilla and sugar until pale and fluffy. Add the cornflour, and whisk until smooth. Pour into the hot milk, and whisk briefly to combine, then microwave for 2 minutes. Whisk well until smooth. Buzz in the microwave for another 1½ minutes, or until a thick paste forms. Whisk madly again, until completely smooth. Press some plastic wrap directly over the surface of the custard, and chill completely – about 2 hours.

Preheat the oven to 210°C (410°F) fan-forced. Have two standard 12-hole muffin tins on standby.

To make the tart shells, roll out the puff pastry into a 30 x 40 cm (12 x 16 inch) rectangle. Sprinkle the ground cinnamon evenly across the surface, and roll snugly into a log. Slice the log into 16 even pieces. Place a piece of pastry into each of 16 muffin holes, with the spiral facing upwards. Tuck the 'tails' underneath, then press and massage the pastry to line each hole completely, with a bit of overhang to make up for shrinkage.

Fill each pastry shell with about a tablespoonful of the custard, and bake for about 30 minutes until the pastry is beautifully golden brown and the custard dotted with black spots. Remove from the oven. Gently remove the tarts from the muffin tin, and cool on a wire rack.

Just before serving, sprinkle each tart with a bit more cinnamon. These keep well in a cake tin for up to 5 days if stored in the refrigerator. Just refresh them in the oven for 10 minutes at 170°C (325°F) fan-forced if you want to eat them warm.

Malaysian Ants' Nest Cake

This is a simple tea cake I grew up eating. The curious tunnel-like structures form from its being cooked with only the bottom element of the oven, giving rise to its other name – honeycomb cake. It has the luscious flavour of caramelised sugar and a lovely springy texture.

FEEDS 10–12

INGREDIENTS

210 g (7½ oz/scant 1 cup) sugar
290 ml (10 fl oz) water
80 g (2¾ oz) butter
6 eggs
160 g (5½ oz/½ cup)
  condensed milk
180 g (6½ oz/1¼ cups) plain
  (all-purpose) flour, sifted
1½ teaspoons baking powder,
  sifted

METHOD

The cake batter starts with a caramel. Combine the sugar and only 2 tablespoons of the 290 ml (10 fl oz) water in a medium, heavy-based saucepan. Mix with a metal spoon to partially dissolve the sugar, then bring to the boil. Do not stir again, but allow the sugar to caramelise until a golden colour. After this, watch and concentrate as it develops into a deep golden brown – blink and it will literally be black, smoking and unsalvageable. When it reaches that ideal colour, immediately turn off the heat, and very carefully add the remaining 250 ml (9 fl oz/ 1 cup) water, in only small amounts at a time, until it has all been used. The caramel will spit and swell violently, so stand well back in between. Add the butter, and whisk until it has melted and combined. Set aside to cool.

Preheat the oven to 180°C (350°F), but ONLY the bottom element. Grease and flour the side of a 20 cm (8 inch) round cake tin. Line the bottom with baking paper.

In a medium mixing bowl, whisk the eggs and condensed milk until combined. Add the flour and baking powder, and whisk until smooth. Add the caramel–butter mixture, and whisk until combined – it will be very runny, but don't be concerned.

Pour the mixture into the prepared tin, and allow to rest for 5 minutes so the bubbles can develop. Bake for 1 hour, or until an inserted skewer comes out clean. Cool the cake in the tin for 5 minutes, before turning it out onto a wire rack to cool completely. Slice and serve plain.

Persian Love Cake

Think those golden baklava-ish flavours, but in a moist cake with sticky, dark caramelised sides. This is a cake to make if you are usually bad at making cakes. Two pluses: it uses a muffin method (what I call a 'bung-in-and-stir'), which requires very little to no technique, and is a wonderful gluten-free option.

FEEDS 12

CRUMB BASE
300 g (10½ oz/3 cups) almond meal
185 g (6½ oz/1 cup) raw caster (superfine) sugar
220 g (7¾ oz/1 cup firmly packed) soft brown sugar
120 g (4¼ oz) unsalted butter, melted

CAKE BATTER
2 eggs, lightly beaten
250 g (9 oz/scant 1 cup) natural OR Greek-style yoghurt
⅛ teaspoon salt
1 teaspoon ground cardamom
2 teaspoons rosewater
25 saffron threads
3 tablespoons flaked almonds
3 tablespoons pistachio nut kernels, roughly chopped

TO DECORATE (OPTIONAL)
Unsprayed edible rose petals

TO SERVE
500 g (1 lb 2 oz/2 cups) Greek-style yoghurt

METHOD
Preheat the oven to 170°C (325°F) fan-forced. Grease the ring of a 24 cm (9½ inch) springform tin, then line with strips of baking paper. Turn the base upside down, so it no longer has a lip. Place a piece of baking paper over it, then clamp the ring around it to secure.

To make the crumb base, combine the almond meal, caster sugar, brown sugar and butter in a large mixing bowl, and rub together until you have an even, sandy consistency. Divide the mixture in two, and tip half into the prepared tin. Using the back of a spoon or a spatula, press the crumb mixture evenly over the bottom of the tin.

To make the cake batter, add the eggs, yoghurt, salt, cardamom, rosewater and saffron to the remaining crumb mixture and whisk until there are no lumps. Pour over the crumb base and sprinkle the flaked almonds and pistachio nuts over the top. Bake for about 20 minutes until golden and fully risen – you will know because the top will probably crack a little. If the top is colouring too quickly, cover with foil, then bake for a further 20 minutes. The centre of the cake should spring back when pressed gently. Cool completely, before removing from the tin and cutting to serve.

Lovely decoration ideas are edible rose petals, sliced fresh figs and a very light dusting of icing sugar. Serve with a dollop of Greek-style yoghurt.

Brutti Ma Buoni – Ugly but Good

I first heard of these when my old mate Julie Goodwin cooked them on *MasterChef Australia* many moons ago, and I remember just loving the honesty of the name. A few years later I filmed a story with an almond grower in South Australia, and she served these up for afternoon tea. After that, I was hooked – a wonderful way to use up extra egg whites and a surplus of almonds. There are so many recipes floating around for this; some are more a crunchy meringue embedded with nuts, but I love mine chewy, so this is how you do it ...

MAKES ABOUT 20 BISCUITS

INGREDIENTS
200 g (7 oz) egg whites (about 6)
Generous pinch of salt
280 g (10 oz) caster (superfine) sugar
1 teaspoon vanilla extract OR vanilla essence
¼ teaspoon ground cinnamon OR 1 teaspoon Dutch process cocoa powder (both optional)
250 g (9 oz) toasted almonds OR hazelnuts, roughly chopped (see first paragraph of Basic Nut Praline method on page 100)

METHOD
Preheat the oven to 150°C (300°F) fan-forced. Line two or three baking trays with baking paper.

Combine the egg whites and salt in a large bowl, and whisk with an electric mixer on high speed until soft peaks form. Add the sugar, a tablespoon at a time, whisking well between each addition, until you have stiff, glossy peaks. Stir in the vanilla, cinnamon and nuts.

Dollop tablespoonsful of the mixture onto the prepared baking trays, leaving a 4 cm (1½ inch) space between each one. Bake for about 30 minutes until the biscuits are pale brown. If you'd like your biscuits to be completely crisp, bake for a further 15 minutes.

Cool completely on the tray before storing them in an airtight container. These will keep well for up to a week.

Peaches Baked with Amaretti

The single most important thing that characterises great Italian fare is its deep respect for simplicity. When you use only a few ingredients, the eating experience is so honest and filled with such clarity that it's hard not to get emotional about it. For all the impatient bakers/ dessert makers out there, you'll be happy with this one.

FEEDS 4

INGREDIENTS

4 peaches, halved & stones removed
    (not a clingstone variety)
16 amaretti biscuits
110 g (3¾ oz/½ cup firmly packed)
    soft brown sugar
8 x 2 cm (¾ inch) butter cubes
    (about 20 g/1 oz) butter)

TO SERVE

½ quantity Yoghurt Mascarpone
    Cream (see page 206)
    OR Crème Chantilly OR
    Vanilla Crème Fraîche OR
    Vanilla Sour Cream (for all
    three, see page 203)
1 tablespoon aged balsamic vinegar
    (optional)

METHOD

Preheat the oven to 180°C (350°F) fan-forced.

Pack all the peach halves, cut side up, into an ovenproof dish. Roughly crush two amaretti biscuits into the centre of each one. Sprinkle the brown sugar over the amaretti, dividing it evenly among the peach halves, then top each peach half with a cube of butter.

Bake for 10–20 minutes until the peaches are slightly caramelised on top. Serve immediately with your choice of dolloping cream and a dash of aged balsamic vinegar.

Upside-Down Cherry Polenta Cake with Balsamic Caramel

This is a gorgeously hearty number that's good for those of you who'd like to take the cake out of the oven and call it a day, without more fussing about with layers or icing. The balsamic caramel is truly to die for, and alone is stunning over ice cream or with custard and poached fruit. You can replace the cherries with pineapple, pears, poached quinces, plums, peaches, apples – anything with a bit of acidity is best.

FEEDS 12–14

CAKE BATTER
600–700 g (1 lb 5 oz–1 lb 9 oz) fresh OR frozen cherries, pitted
3 eggs, separated
¼ teaspoon cream of tartar
220 g (7¾ oz/1 cup) caster (superfine) sugar
120 g (4¼ oz) unsalted butter, softened
¼ teaspoon salt
1 teaspoon vanilla extract OR vanilla essence
185 g (6½ oz/1¼ cups) plain (all-purpose) flour, sifted
50 g (1¾ oz/¼ cup) fine polenta (cornmeal)
2 teaspoons baking powder, sifted
Finely grated zest of 1 lemon
125 ml (4 fl oz/½ cup) milk

BALSAMIC CARAMEL
90 g (3¼ oz) unsalted butter
110 g (3¾ oz/½ cup firmly packed) soft brown sugar
3 tablespoons balsamic vinegar

TO SERVE
1 quantity Yoghurt Mascarpone Cream (see page 206) OR Crème Chantilly OR Vanilla Sour Cream OR Vanilla Crème Fraîche (for all three, see page 203)

METHOD
Line the side and bottom of a 24 cm (9½ inch) round cake tin with baking paper. Arrange a single layer of the cherries over the bottom of the cake tin. Set aside.

To make the balsamic caramel, combine the butter, brown sugar and balsamic vinegar in a small saucepan. Bring to the boil, then reduce and simmer for 2 minutes. Drizzle a few spoonfuls over the cherries in the bottom of the cake tin, and reserve the rest for serving.

Preheat the oven to 160°C (315°F) fan-forced.

So you don't have to clean your beaters in between, whisk the egg whites and cream of tartar first – in a medium mixing bowl with an electric mixer on high speed until medium peaks form. Add half the sugar, but only 1 tablespoon at a time, whisking well between each addition. Set aside.

In a separate medium mixing bowl, beat the remaining sugar, butter, salt and vanilla with an electric mixer on high speed until pale and fluffy. Add the egg yolks one at a time, beating well between each addition. Fold in the flour, polenta and baking powder, then the lemon zest and milk.

Whisk in one-third of the egg white mixture to loosen, before adding the remainder and stirring gently with a whisk to combine. Pour over the cherries in the prepared tin. Bake for about 1 hour, or until an inserted skewer comes out clean. Cool the cake in the tin only until warm, then carefully turn it over onto a serving plate. Pour the balsamic caramel over the top, so the cake is nice and glossy, and serve immediately with your choice of dolloping cream.

Chiffon Boston Cream Pie

Curiously, a Boston cream pie is really not a pie but a cake. What defines it as a Boston cream pie is the pairing of the custard or cream layers with a chocolate frosting of some kind, rather than the type of cake used. In this case, it's the lightest, spongiest of cakes, filled with layers of vanilla custard, then finished with cascades of chocolate ganache – soft, oozy, delicious and usually inhaled within minutes!

FEEDS 12–14

ORANGE CHIFFON CAKE

5 eggs, separated + 2 extra
    egg whites
½ teaspoon cream of tartar
150 g (5½ oz/⅔ cup) caster
    (superfine) sugar
80 ml (2½ fl oz/⅓ cup) grapeseed
    oil OR vegetable oil
Finely grated zest of 1 orange
80 ml (2½ fl oz/⅓ cup) orange juice
100 ml (3½ fl oz) tinned
    coconut milk
150 g (5½ oz/1 cup) plain
    (all-purpose) flour, sifted
2 teaspoons baking powder, sifted
Pinch of salt

TO FINISH

1 quantity chilled Crème Pâtissiére
    (see page 204)
1 quantity Dark OR Milk Chocolate
    Ganache (see page 202)

METHOD

Preheat the oven to 170°C (325°F) fan-forced. Have a 25 cm (10 inch) angel food cake tin on standby. Do not grease or use a non-stick tin – for the chiffon to rise properly, sticky sides are exactly what the mixture needs to climb and sustain the impressive height.

To make the chiffon cake, first make a meringue. In a large bowl, whisk the 7 egg whites and cream of tartar with an electric mixer on high speed until medium peaks form. Add half the caster sugar, a tablespoon at a time, whisking well between additions, until this portion of the sugar has been used up and the meringue is glossy with stiff peaks. Set aside.

Next, whisk the egg yolks and remaining sugar in a medium mixing bowl until pale and thick. Add the grapeseed oil, orange zest and juice, and coconut milk, and whisk until combined. Add the flour, baking powder and salt, and whisk until just smooth. Spoon one-third of the meringue mixture into the egg yolk mixture, and whisk until combined. Fold in the remaining meringue with a whisk, taking care to get rid of any small pockets of egg white.

Pour the mixture into the angel food cake tin, smooth out the surface and bake for 30–40 minutes, or until an inserted skewer comes out clean. Immediately invert the cake tin when it comes out of the oven, and cool the cake completely before turning it out – about 2 hours. To do this, run a knife around the inner and outer sides of the tin, and you'll find that the cake will release easily. Slide the knife along the bottom of the tin to free the cake completely.

To assemble, carefully slice the cake into three layers and sandwich the layers together with the custard. Pour the ganache over the cake, allowing it to cascade down the side – if it is too runny, allow it to set a little before attempting again. You can then manipulate the cascading more by pushing it around with a spatula. Surprisingly, this cake keeps very well and will stay nice and moist for about 4 days, but it never lasts that long!

Cheat's Sour Cherry Strudel with Lemon Cream

My old mates Boof and Charlie made a version of this at a dinner party many moons ago, when they were just teenagers (sigh) and I was in my early twenties, and I've loved it since. It's an excellent one to try if you're not a gifted baker or in a rush because, really, you just have to brush and layer some ready-made filo with butter, roll very simply, put things in it, and stick it in the oven. The other fab thing about it is that you can change up the fruit or even fill it with something savoury.

FEEDS 8

INGREDIENTS

8 sheets ready-made filo pastry

50 g (1¾ oz) butter, melted

2 pink lady OR granny smith apples, peeled, cored & cut into 1 cm (½ inch) dice

680 g (1 lb 8 oz) jar pitted morello cherries in light syrup, drained

60 g (2¼ oz/½ cup) walnuts, toasted (see first paragraph of Basic Nut Praline method on page 100)

40 g (1½ oz/¼ cup) currants

1 tablespoon Frangelico liqueur OR kirsch

55 g (2 oz/¼ cup) caster (superfine) sugar OR soft brown sugar

3 teaspoons plain (all-purpose) flour

½–1 teaspoon ground cinnamon

TO SERVE

Icing (confectioners') sugar, to dust

1 quantity Lemon Cream OR Vanilla Sour Cream OR Vanilla Crème Fraîche (for all three, see page 203)

METHOD

Preheat the oven to 180°C (350°F) fan-forced.

To make the strudel, lay a sheet of the filo pastry on a large baking tray lined with a sheet of baking paper, and brush with a generous amount of the melted butter. Lay another sheet on top, and repeat. Continue in this way until all the filo has been used. Set aside.

Combine the apples, cherries, walnuts, currants, Frangelico, sugar, flour and cinnamon in a medium mixing bowl, and toss gently with clean hands to mix the ingredients evenly.

Tip the mixture across the centre of the filo sheets, leaving a 7 cm (2¾ inch) border on each side. Fold both sides inwards, then roll into a sausage to enclose the filling. If it's a bit of a mess, unwrap the pastry, pop all the bits that have fallen out back into the centre and have another go, as the filo is fairly robust.

Carefully shimmy the strudel so that it's positioned across the centre of the baking tray, then brush the surface with more of the melted butter. Bake for about 30 minutes until a deep golden brown, so all the layers are cooked through. Leave to cool for at least 30 minutes before serving.

Dust with icing sugar just before serving with your choice of dolloping cream.

Turkish Delight

It's really nice to be able to make a basic like this because the practice feels ancient. When you've been stirring over a hot stove for a while and there's not really any gadget that can fast-forward things, you kind of just abandon yourself to the old-worldliness of the act, and wind up having romantic thoughts such as wondering who the first person was ever to make Turkish delight ...

MAKES ABOUT 80 PIECES

SUGAR SYRUP
580 g (1 lb 5 oz/2⅔ cups) sugar
175 g (6 oz/½ cup) honey
Pinch of cream of tartar
125 ml (4 fl oz/½ cup) water

STARCH MIXTURE
125 g (4½ oz/1 cup) wheaten
   cornflour (cornstarch), see note
   on page 33
125 g (4½ oz/1 cup) icing
   (confectioners') sugar
1 teaspoon cream of tartar
625 ml (21½ fl oz/2½ cups) water
15 g (½ oz) gelatine sheets,
   soaked in a bowl of cool
   water for 1 minute

BITS & PIECES
1 tablespoon rosewater
¼ teaspoon pink or red food
   colouring
70 g (2½ oz/½ cup) toasted
   pistachio nut kernels, roughly
   chopped (see first paragraph
   of Basic Nut Praline method
   on page 100)

DREDGING POWDER
125 g (4½ oz/1 cup) icing
   (confectioners') sugar
60 g (2 oz/½ cup wheaten cornflour
   (cornstarch)

METHOD
Line a 20 x 30 cm (8 x 12 inch) baking tray with baking paper. If you want to be extra cautious, spray the paper with a little cooking oil spray, but wipe off any excess.

To make the sugar syrup, combine the sugar, honey and cream of tartar in a medium–large saucepan. Add the 125 ml (4 fl oz/½ cup) water. Stir with a metal spoon until smooth, then bring to the boil without disturbing the liquid again. Boil for 10–15 minutes until very little to no steam is rising from the syrup and the mixture turns slightly more golden.

While the sugar syrup is boiling, make the starch mixture by combining the cornflour, icing sugar, cream of tartar and the 625 ml (21½ fl oz/2½ cups) water in a medium saucepan. Cook over medium heat, whisking continuously, until you have a thick, smooth paste. Turn off the heat, but leave the saucepan on the stove.

When the syrup is ready, carefully pour it into the starch mixture, and whisk until smooth. Return the saucepan to medium heat. Cook for 5–10 minutes, whisking continuously, until the mixture is very thick. Squeeze all the water out of the gelatine sheets, and add the gelatine to the mixture with the rosewater, food colouring and pistachios. Stir well, making sure the ingredients are combined and the gelatine has dissolved, then pour into the prepared tray. It will take about 5 hours for the mixture to chill in the fridge and set completely.

To make the dredging powder, sift the icing sugar and cornflour into a medium mixing bowl to combine well. Return the powder to the sieve, and shake generously over the slab of Turkish delight, then flip it over onto a cutting board. Carefully peel off the baking paper. Dust more of the dredging powder over the bottom of the slab (which is now facing upwards), and slice into 2 cm (¾ inch) squares. Between slices, rinse the knife under hot water, then dry. Toss the Turkish delight in more of the dredging powder. Store in an airtight container, keeping the layers separated with baking paper. These will keep well for up to a month in a cool place.

chapter eight

TRUSTY TEA CAKES

Mum's Apple Custard Cake

Mum's been making this cake for aeons – I call it the 'smile maker'. You can't possibly *not* win with apples and custard! If making the custard from scratch is an idea you scoff at, you can of course (like my mum) go the instant powdered type, but it will cause me to die a little bit on the inside.

FEEDS 12–14

CUSTARD
350 ml (12 fl oz) milk
4 eggs
150 g (5½ oz/⅔ cup) caster
    (superfine) sugar
1½ teaspoons vanilla extract
    OR vanilla essence
2 tablespoons wheaten cornflour
    (cornstarch), see note on
    page 33

CAKE BATTER
250 g (9 oz) unsalted butter,
    softened
335 g (11¾ oz/1½ cups) caster
    (superfine) sugar
1½ teaspoons vanilla extract
    OR vanilla essence
½ teaspoon salt
1 teaspoon finely grated lemon zest
6 eggs
125 ml (4 fl oz/½ cup) sour cream
335 g (11¾ oz/2¼ cups) plain
    (all-purpose) flour, sifted
3½ teaspoons baking powder, sifted
3 pink lady OR granny smith apples,
    peeled, cored & cut into 3 mm
    (⅛ inch) slices
1 teaspoon ground cinnamon

TO SERVE
1 quantity Crème Chantilly OR
    Vanilla Sour Cream OR Vanilla
    Crème Fraîche (for all three,
    see page 203)

METHOD
To make the custard, microwave the milk in a heatproof bowl for 2 minutes on the highest setting. Meanwhile, whisk the eggs, sugar and vanilla in a medium mixing bowl until pale and thick. Add the cornflour, and whisk until smooth. Pour this into the hot milk, and whisk to combine. Buzz in the microwave for 2 minutes on the highest setting. Whisk until smooth, and microwave in 1-minute bursts until you have a thick paste. Press some plastic wrap directly on the surface of the custard, to prevent a skin from forming, and set aside.

Preheat the oven to 170°C (325°F) fan-forced. Grease the ring of a 22–24 cm (8½–9½ inch) springform tin, then turn the base upside down, so it no longer has a lip. Place a piece of baking paper over it, then clamp the ring around it to secure.

To make the cake batter, combine the butter, sugar, vanilla, salt and lemon zest in a medium mixing bowl, and beat with an electric mixer until pale and fluffy. Add the eggs one at a time, beating well between each addition. Whisk in the sour cream by hand, then fold through the flour and baking powder in two or three batches.

Spread half the cake batter over the bottom of the prepared tin, add a middle layer of the custard and then the remaining batter. Arrange the apple slices in concentric circles over the top, sprinkle with the cinnamon and bake for 40 minutes, or until an inserted skewer comes out clean. Slide a knife around the edge of the tin, before releasing the ring and carefully sliding the cake onto a wire rack. Cool completely, before cutting and serving with your choice of dolloping cream.

Olive Oil Rosemary Apricot Cake

For the non-sweet tooths out there, this one's for you. This savoury combination of olive oil, rosemary and lemon in a cake is just sensational and so wonderfully Mediterranean. If you are desperate to make this outside of apricot season, apricot halves tinned in syrup make a good substitute.

FEEDS 10–12

INGREDIENTS

5 eggs, separated
165 g (5¾ oz/¾ cup) caster (superfine) sugar + 1 tablespoon, to sprinkle
¼ teaspoon salt
185 ml (6 fl oz/¾ cup) olive oil
Finely grated zest & juice of 1 lemon
1 teaspoon finely chopped fresh rosemary
150 g (5½ oz/1 cup) plain (all-purpose) flour, sifted
10 apricots, halved & stones removed, OR tinned apricot halves, drained

TO SERVE

1 quantity Vanilla Sour Cream OR Vanilla Crème Fraîche (for both, see page 203) OR Yoghurt Mascarpone Cream (see page 206)

METHOD

Preheat the oven to 170°C (325°F) fan-forced. Grease the ring of a 20–22 cm (8–8½ inch) springform tin, then turn the base upside down, so it no longer has a lip. Place a piece of baking paper over it, then clamp the ring around it to secure.

To make the cake, in a medium mixing bowl, whisk the egg whites with an electric mixer on medium speed until just foamy. Add only 55 g (2 oz/¼ cup) of the caster sugar in two batches, whisking well between each addition, until soft peaks form. Set aside.

Combine the egg yolks, remaining caster sugar and salt in a medium mixing bowl, and whisk with an electric mixer on high speed until pale and thick. Gradually drizzle in the olive oil, whisking on high speed until all of it has been used. Add the lemon zest and juice, rosemary and flour, and stir with a whisk until just combined. Whisk in one-third of the egg whites to loosen the mixture, then add the remainder and stir very gently with the whisk until combined.

Pour the batter into the prepared cake tin, and arrange the apricot halves in concentric circles on top, working from the outside in. Sprinkle the extra tablespoon of caster sugar evenly over the surface, and bake for about 50 minutes, or until an inserted skewer comes out clean. Rest the cake in the tin for 5 minutes, before releasing the ring and sliding the cake onto a wire rack to cool. Rest for about 30 minutes, before slicing and serving with your choice of dolloping cream – warm works for this cake!

Fig, Coconut & Orange Syrup Cake

This is a stunning tea cake, rich with the flavour of coconut, sticky figs and a bright orange syrup to bring it all together. The mild sharpness of the Yoghurt Mascarpone Cream topping is fabulous for cutting through the sweetness of the syrup and generally fabulous as an alternative to Crème Chantilly (see page 203).

FEEDS 12–14

INGREDIENTS

150 g (5½ oz) unsalted butter, softened
175 g (6 oz) caster (superfine) sugar
1 teaspoon vanilla extract OR vanilla essence
¼ teaspoon salt
3 eggs
65 g (2½ oz/¼ cup) sour cream
175 g (6 oz) plain (all-purpose) flour, sifted
2½ teaspoons baking powder, sifted
80 ml (2½ fl oz/⅓ cup) milk
80 g (2¾ oz) dried figs, chopped
65 g (2½ oz/1 cup) dried shredded coconut

ORANGE SYRUP

Finely grated zest of 1 orange
80 ml (2½ fl oz/⅓ cup) freshly squeezed orange juice
Juice of 1 lemon
75 g (2½ oz/⅓ cup) sugar

TO SERVE

Candied orange zest (see note), to decorate
1 quantity Yoghurt Mascarpone Cream (see page 206)

METHOD

Preheat the oven to 160°C (315°F) fan-forced. Grease and flour a 25 cm (10 inch) kugelhopf (bundt) tin.

To make the batter, combine the butter, sugar, vanilla and salt in a medium mixing bowl. Beat with an electric mixer on high speed until pale and fluffy. Add the eggs one at a time, beating well between each addition. Gently stir in the sour cream with a whisk, then add the flour and baking powder, continuing to stir with a whisk until combined. Fold in the milk, figs and coconut, then transfer the mixture to the prepared tin.

Bake for about 45 minutes, or until an inserted skewer comes out clean. Remove from the oven and rest for a few minutes, before turning out the cake to cool on a wire rack sitting on a baking tray.

Meanwhile, make the orange syrup. Combine the orange zest, orange and lemon juices and sugar in a small saucepan. Stir on a simmer until the sugar has dissolved. Pour over the cake while both the cake and the syrup are hot.

When the cake has cooled completely, transfer it to a serving plate and decorate with the candied orange zest. Serve with the Yoghurt Mascarpone Cream.

NOTE

To make candied orange zest, please see page 147. Use the candied lime zest recipe, but substitute the lime with the zest of 1 orange.

Rustic Pear, Hazelnut & Prune Cake

There's something about the generosity of the whole pears in this cake that's incredibly inviting. A luscious, moist tea cake that makes a beautiful rustic centrepiece for an afternoon tea get-together.

FEEDS 12–14

POACHED PEARS

7 small corella OR 4 beurre bosc pears (pick ones that are the same size and shape)
625 ml (21½ fl oz/2½ cups) water
220 g (7¾ oz/1 cup) sugar
1 teaspoon vanilla bean paste OR vanilla extract

CAKE BATTER

125 g (4½ oz) unsalted butter, softened
165 g (5¾ oz/¾ cup) caster (superfine) sugar
¼ teaspoon salt
3 eggs
80 ml (2½ fl oz/⅓ cup) sour cream
200 g (7 oz/1⅓ cups) plain (all-purpose) flour
1¾ teaspoons baking powder
55 g (2 oz/½ cup) hazelnut meal
70 g (2½ oz/⅓ cup) pitted prunes, roughly sliced
2 tablespoons milk
Finely grated zest of ½ lemon
40 g (1½ oz/¼ cup) hazelnuts, roughly chopped

TO SERVE

1 quantity of any of the dolloping creams (see page 203)

METHOD

To poach the pears, peel but leave whole with the stems intact when using corellas; if using beurre bosc, peel, then halve them lengthways. Combine the pears, water, sugar and vanilla in a medium saucepan, and bring to the boil. Reduce the heat, cover and simmer for 30 minutes until the pears are tender. With a slotted spoon, carefully transfer the pears to a colander, and allow them to drain and cool. Meanwhile, boil the poaching syrup until its volume has reduced by half. Set aside to cool completely.

Preheat the oven to 170°C (325°F) fan-forced. Grease the ring of a 24–25 cm (9½–10 inch) springform tin, then turn the base upside down, so it no longer has a lip. Place a piece of baking paper over it, then clamp the ring around it to secure.

To make the cake batter, combine the butter, sugar and salt in a medium mixing bowl, and beat with an electric mixer on the highest speed until pale and fluffy. Add the eggs one at a time, beating well between each addition. Add the sour cream, and whisk until combined, then fold in the flour, baking powder, hazelnut meal, prunes, milk and lemon zest.

Pour the batter into the prepared tin, then press the corella pears, stems up, around the edge of the cake. If using beurre boscs, press them cut side up into the batter, so they radiate in a circle, with the narrow tip of the pears at the centre of the cake. Sprinkle the hazelnuts on top, and bake for about 1½ hours, or until an inserted skewer comes out clean.

When the cake comes out of the oven, rest for 5 minutes, then run a paring knife around the side of the cake and release it from the tin. Carefully slide the cake onto a wire rack to cool completely, before transferring it to a serving plate. Brush generously with the pear syrup, and serve with your choice of dolloping cream.

Blueberry Lemon Syrup Cake

Lemon syrup cake is surely one of the most loved cakes in the world. I once had a tub of slightly neglected blueberries in the fridge and happened to be making this old favourite – the combination was an instant hit with the family. This is one of very few cakes that's fabulous to eat shortly after it's out of the oven (yes, in the majority of cases, that's a fallacy) – warm with a dollop of rich cream, it's the best kind of old-fashioned magic.

FEEDS 10–12

INGREDIENTS

125 g (4½ oz) unsalted butter, softened
160 g (5¾ oz/¾ cup) caster (superfine) sugar
¼ teaspoon salt
Finely grated zest of 1 lemon
2 large eggs
60 ml (2 fl oz/¼ cup) milk
165 g (5¾ oz) plain (all-purpose) flour
2 teaspoons baking powder
80 g (2¾ oz/½ cup) fresh OR frozen blueberries

LEMON SYRUP

60 ml (2 fl oz/¼ cup) lemon juice
90 g (3¼ oz/¾ cup) icing (confectioners') sugar

TO SERVE

1 quantity Vanilla Sour Cream OR Vanilla Crème Fraîche (for both, see page 203) OR Yoghurt Mascarpone Cream (see page 206)

METHOD

Preheat the oven to 160°C (315°F) fan-forced. Grease the ring of a 20 cm (8 inch) springform tin, then turn the base upside down, so it no longer has a lip. Place a piece of baking paper over it, then clamp the ring around it to secure.

To make the cake batter, combine the butter, sugar, salt and zest in a medium mixing bowl, and beat with an electric mixer on high speed until pale and fluffy. Add the eggs one at a time, beating well between each addition. Add the milk, and whisk until combined. Fold in the flour and baking powder until combined.

Pour the batter into the prepared tin, and dot the surface of the mixture with the blueberries. Bake for about 40 minutes, or until an inserted skewer comes out clean. Rest the cake for about 5 minutes, before running a paring knife around the edge of the cake to release the ring, then sliding it onto a wire rack sitting over a baking tray.

Meanwhile, make the syrup. Combine the lemon juice and icing sugar in a small saucepan over medium heat, and stir until the sugar has dissolved. While the cake is still hot, pierce small holes all over the surface with a skewer, and pour the hot syrup slowly and as evenly as you can over the cake.

Allow to cool for at least 20 minutes before cutting. If it's still hot as opposed to warm, the cake will not cut well but, if you can't wait and don't mind, go ahead! Serve with your choice of dolloping cream.

Charlie's Currant Tea Cake

This is literally a cake made with tea, not just a cake to have with tea – although they are terrific together. For such a simple thing to whip up, it always amazes me how moreish the outcome is, especially when warmed up in the toaster and eaten with slathers of salted butter. You can change the character of the cake by using a different tea, as long as it's always black – Earl Grey is one of my favourites.

FEEDS 10–12

INGREDIENTS
140 g (5 oz/1 cup) currants
    OR 170 g (6 oz) sultanas
    (golden raisins)
220 g (7¾ oz/1 cup) caster
    (superfine) sugar
250 ml (9 fl oz/1 cup) strong hot
    black tea
300 g (10½ oz/2 cups) plain
    (all-purpose) flour
3 teaspoons baking powder
½ teaspoon salt

METHOD
Combine the currants, sugar and hot tea in a medium mixing bowl, and leave to soak for about 4 hours or overnight if possible.

Preheat the oven to 160°C (315°F) fan-forced. Grease and flour a 25 x 12 x 6 cm (10 x 4½ x 2½ inch) loaf tin.

Add the flour, baking powder and salt to the bowl with the currants, and mix until smooth. Transfer the batter to the prepared tin, and bake for about 1 hour, or until an inserted skewer comes out clean. Turn out onto a wire rack to cool a little, before slicing it while warm and eating with salted butter.

Silken Pear Cake

So little flour is used in this recipe that what comes out of the oven is almost a whisper of a cake – fairy light and studded with chunks of silky pear.

FEEDS 10–12

INGREDIENTS

3 eggs
130 g (4½ oz) caster (superfine) sugar
1 teaspoon vanilla extract OR vanilla essence
35 g (1¼ oz/¼ cup) plain (all-purpose) flour, sifted
30 g (1 oz/¼ cup) wheaten cornflour (cornstarch), sifted (see note on page 33)
1 teaspoon baking powder, sifted
Pinch of salt
90 g (3¼ oz) unsalted butter, melted
3 ripe pears, peeled, cored & cut into 2 cm (¾ inch) dice

TO SERVE

1 quantity Crème Chantilly (see page 203) OR Yoghurt Mascarpone Cream (see page 206)

METHOD

Preheat the oven to 170°C (325°F) fan-forced. Grease the ring of a 24 cm (9½ inch) springform tin, then turn the base upside down, so it no longer has a lip. Place a piece of baking paper over it, then clamp the ring around it to secure.

Combine the eggs, sugar and vanilla in a mixing bowl, and whisk with an electric mixer on high speed until the mixture is triple its original volume. Using a whisk, gently fold in the flour, cornflour, baking powder and salt until smooth. Add the melted butter, and fold with the whisk until combined. Tilt the bowl to make sure you are reaching right to the bottom, where remnants of melted butter might be sitting.

Pour the mixture into the prepared tin, then drop the chunks of diced pear evenly over the surface. Don't worry if there are a few pieces peeking through the top of the batter.

Bake for about 45 minutes, or until an inserted skewer comes out clean. The cake will balloon up when cooking, then collapse a bit after cooling, so don't have a meltdown when this happens. Cool completely in the tin, before sliding a paring knife around the edge of the cake to release the ring. Carefully slide the cake onto a serving plate, leaving it on the baking paper because the texture is very delicate. Serve with your choice of dolloping cream.

Lumberjack Cake

This cake has serious currency in a baking repertoire. If, in your lifetime, you learn how to make very few cakes, this should definitely be one of them. Its appearance is understated, with all its moist, dense, puddingy goodness hiding under a golden coconut caramel crust and sides so deeply caramelised that you could almost mistake them for being burnt ... but no. Dive inside and you have apples and dates, something wholesome and robust, perhaps even a cake cousin to the Anzac biscuit (see page 120).

FEEDS UP TO 16

DATE & APPLE MIXTURE
300 g (10½ oz/1¾ cups) pitted dates
1½ teaspoons bicarbonate of soda (baking soda)
375 ml (13 fl oz/1½ cups) boiling water
3 apples, peeled, cored & cut into 1 cm (½ inch) dice

CAKE BATTER
180 g (6½ oz) unsalted butter, softened
330 g (11½ oz/1½ cups) caster (superfine) sugar
1½ teaspoons vanilla extract OR vanilla essence
½ teaspoon salt
2 eggs
330 g (11½ oz/2¼ cups) plain (all-purpose) flour, sifted

TOPPING
100 g (3½ oz) unsalted butter
150 g (5½ oz/⅔ cup) firmly packed soft brown sugar
180 ml (6 fl oz/¾ cup) milk
150 g (5½ oz/about 1 cup) dried shredded coconut
¼ teaspoon salt

METHOD
Preheat the oven to 160°C (315°F) fan-forced. Turn the base of a 24–25 cm (9½–10 inch) springform tin upside down, so it no longer has a lip. Place a piece of baking paper over the base, then clamp the ring around it to secure. Grease the ring, then cut strips of baking paper to line the side with a 2 cm (¾ inch) overhang.

To make the date and apple mixture, combine the dates, bicarbonate of soda and boiling water in a medium mixing bowl – it should fizz up a bit. Stir and allow to sit for about 15 minutes, then transfer to a food processor and pulse into a rough purée. Stir in the apples, to cool the mixture slightly, and set aside.

To make the cake batter, combine the butter, sugar, vanilla and salt in a medium mixing bowl, and beat with an electric mixer on the highest speed until light and fluffy. Add the eggs one at a time, beating well between each addition, then fold in the flour. Add the reserved date and apple mixture, and fold to combine. Pour the mixture into the prepared tin. Bake for 50–60 minutes, or until an inserted skewer comes out clean. Remove the cake from the oven, and carefully set on a heatproof surface. Do not turn off the oven.

Meanwhile, combine all the topping ingredients in a small non-stick saucepan over medium heat. Cook and stir for about 5 minutes until the mixture is golden, sticky and only the slightest bit runny. Gently spread evenly over the top of the cooked cake, and return to the oven to bake for another 30 minutes, or until a deep golden brown.

Allow the cake to cool in the tin for 5 minutes, before releasing the ring and sliding the cake onto a wire rack. Cool completely, before cutting with a serrated knife and serving.

Avocado Loaf with Raspberry Glaze

I bet you're thinking, 'Surely the flavour of the avocado will be lost. And surely the raspberry glaze will be too overpowering.' But no – the two sit simply but beautifully together in every mouthful. A fab recipe for breathing a second life into those sad-looking avos sitting in the fruit bowl.

FEEDS UP TO 10

INGREDIENTS

2 eggs, separated
165 g (5¾ oz/¾ cup) caster (superfine) sugar
185 ml (6 fl oz/¾ cup) avocado purée
75 g (2½ oz) unsalted butter, softened
60 ml (2 fl oz/¼ cup) milk
1 teaspoon vanilla extract OR vanilla essence
185 g (6½ oz/1¼ cups) plain (all-purpose) flour, sifted
1 teaspoon baking powder, sifted
¼ teaspoon salt

RASPBERRY GLAZE

40 g (1½ oz/⅓ cup) fresh OR frozen raspberries
90 g (3¼ oz/¾ cup) pure icing (confectioners') sugar
25 g (1 oz) unsalted butter, cut into 1 cm (½ inch) dice

TO SERVE

1 quantity Vanilla Sour Cream OR Vanilla Crème Fraîche (for both, see page 203)

METHOD

Preheat the oven to 160°C (315°F) fan-forced. Grease and flour a 25 x 12 x 6 cm (10 x 4½ x 2½ inch) loaf tin.

Whisk the egg whites in a medium mixing bowl with an electric mixer on high speed until soft peaks form. Add 2 tablespoons of the 165 g (5¾ oz/¾ cup) caster sugar, a tablespoon at a time, whisking until medium peaks form.

In a separate medium mixing bowl, combine the avocado purée, butter and remaining sugar. Using an electric mixer, beat until light and fluffy. Add the egg yolks one at a time, beating well between each addition, then add the milk and vanilla – don't be concerned if the mixture curdles at this stage. With a whisk, gently stir in the flour, baking powder and salt, then half the egg white mixture. Fold in the remaining egg white mixture until combined.

Pour the batter into the prepared tin, and bake for about 40 minutes, or until an inserted skewer comes out clean. Wait for 1 minute, before turning the cake out onto a wire rack to cool. Cool completely before glazing.

To make the raspberry glaze, combine the raspberries and icing sugar in a small saucepan, and bring to the boil. Stir briefly to ensure that the sugar has dissolved, then carefully blitz with a blender until smooth. Stir in the butter until melted.

Place the cake on a serving plate, and pour the glaze over the top. Serve with your choice of dolloping cream.

chapter nine
MUST-KNOWS

These are your best friends in the kitchen because with them,
you can beautify desserts and elevate flavour. You can also make
them your cover-up accomplices for those times when you need
a plan B or maybe even a plan C!

Rough Puff Pastry

This is a basic you simply cannot do without if you want to get serious about baking. Incredibly versatile, it can be used in sweet dishes as a main feature or to add a crunchy element to a deconstructed dessert. Without altering a thing, you can also use it to make pasties, a beef wellington or a pie top on a stew.

MAKES ABOUT 620 G (1 LB 6 OZ) PASTRY

INGREDIENTS
250 g (9 oz) unsalted butter, chilled
250 g (9 oz/1⅔ cups) plain (all-purpose) flour
1 teaspoon salt
120 ml (4 fl oz/½ cup) cold water

BY MACHINE
To make the rough puff by machine, cut the butter into 2 cm (¾ inch) dice. Combine the butter, flour and salt in a food processor. Pulse for 1–2 seconds until you see the butter has broken down into roughly 1 cm (½ inch) chunks. Tip the mixture into a medium mixing bowl. Drizzle the cold water evenly in concentric circles over the mixture, then gather the crumbs in a circular motion, squeezing them together until you have a rough mass that is mostly sticking together.

BY HAND
To make the rough puff by hand, the butter should be at room temperature. Mix the flour and salt roughly in a large mixing bowl, and break 2 cm (¾ inch) chunks of the butter into it. Grab handfuls of the mixture, and rub between your hands so the chunks break down a little, but marble-sized pieces of butter still remain. Make a well in the centre, pour in the water and gently gather the mixture into a single, crumbly lump – do not knead; instead use a circular gathering motion.

LAMINATING
To laminate the dough, flour your work surface well, place the dough on it and shape into a rectangle, with the longer part placed vertically in front of you. Don't be concerned if the dough looks a crumbly mess of wet and dry bits, as long as it's generally holding together. Begin to roll the dough, so it's just over double in length than it is wide, then fold into thirds. Always pat the sides inwards to make sure you have a nice, uniform rectangle to work before you start the next 'turn'. Turn the dough 90 degrees clockwise, and repeat this process another two times. Rest in the refrigerator for 30 minutes, and you have just made rough puff pastry!

THINGS TO BEAR IN MIND

Before you start rolling, some tips: Work quickly. If you find your pastry is turning room temperature and getting limp, pop it back in the refrigerator for 20 minutes. If the butter softens too much, it will be absorbed by the dough and the layers won't separate or puff properly when baking.

Watch out for a marbled effect as the dough is rolled. If it's not noticeable, you might have overhandled the dough and inadvertently made shortcrust pastry – but don't fret. Keep going. Sometimes it will still turn out; if not, it will still be delicious, just not the exact texture we want. Try again.

The cooking times and temperatures for cooking puff will vary depending on what you're using it for, so follow individual recipes from this stage onwards.

Dark or Milk Chocolate Ganache

To make a dark or milk chocolate ganache, you don't need a recipe. If you just remember the very easy 1:1 weight ratio, you're set. For white chocolate ganache, it's half the amount of cream (1:2 weight ratio) – for example, 50 ml (2 fl oz) cream to 100 g (3½ oz) white chocolate – and follow the same method below.

COVERS A 20–25 CM (8–10 INCH) X 8–10 CM (3¼–4 INCH) CAKE COMFORTABLY

INGREDIENTS

100 ml (3½ fl oz) thin (pouring) OR thickened (whipping) cream
100 g (3½ oz/⅔ cup) dark OR milk chocolate melts (buttons) OR chopped dark OR milk chocolate

METHOD

Microwave the cream and chocolate in a small heatproof bowl for 1 minute on the highest setting, then whisk until smooth. Buzz for another 30 seconds if the chocolate hasn't completely melted, and whisk again. If you prefer, you can heat the cream in a small saucepan until a few small bubbles rise to the surface. Remove from the heat, add the chocolate and whisk until smooth.

If you are finding the ganache very runny and difficult to handle, allow it to cool down for a few minutes and the fats will set a little. However, be careful when you are slathering it all over your desired cake; if you muck about with it too much, you will lose all its glam gloss and wind up with a matte, grainy-looking finish. The flavour will still be ace, so it's just a textural compromise. The shine also diminishes if you refrigerate whatever it is you cover in ganache, so it's best to do it last minute.

Dolloping Creams

With all the different styles of dolloping cream, you should know you don't actually need a recipe. All you want is to remember the ratio. Rule of thumb is icing sugar will always be 10% of the cream amount no matter what. For example, you would mix 30 g (1 oz) icing sugar with 300 ml (10½ fl oz) of cream, then it's generally 1–1½ teaspoons vanilla extract or to taste. With the cultured creams, you could probably add a smidgen more icing sugar to balance the sharpness but, as is, they will be especially perfect for those who prefer things not overly sweet.

MAKES ABOUT 300 ML (10½ FL OZ)

CRÈME CHANTILLY

300 ml (10½ fl oz) thickened (whipping) cream
30 g (1 oz/¼ cup) pure icing (confectioners') sugar OR icing (confectioners') sugar mixture, sifted
1 teaspoon vanilla extract OR vanilla bean paste OR vanilla essence

CRÈME CHANTILLY

This is your most basic, most neutral-tasting cream for dolloping on desserts and decorating cakes. Make sure you don't overwhisk this, or you will split the cream and be on your way to making butter. The only way to remedy this, unfortunately, is to start again from scratch.

Combine the cream, icing sugar and vanilla in a medium mixing bowl, and whisk by hand or with an electric mixer until medium or stiff peaks form. Medium peaks make a nicer texture to dollop and provide moisture to slices of cake. Stiff peaks are more fitting for icing cakes and piping with, as the shape stays put.

LEMON OR ORANGE CREAM

I like to use either of these to bolster the citrus flavour in cakes and desserts. Use the same recipe as for crème Chantilly, but swap out the vanilla for 1 teaspoon finely grated lemon or orange zest.

VANILLA SOUR CREAM OR VANILLA CRÈME FRAÎCHE

Sour cream and crème fraîche are the next options. Both of these are cultured creams, so have a desirable sharpness that is great for cutting through sweet things, but they differ in fat content.

Sour cream has a lower fat content, which means it does not whip. It's structurally more similar to yoghurt, so you get a more runny finish that will separate if left for a while. Sour cream is also easier to find.

Crème fraîche, on the other hand, can be whipped because of its higher fat content, but it will only be to soft to medium peaks.

To make Vanilla Sour Cream, use the crème Chantilly recipe, but swap out the cream for sour cream, and stir with a spoon to combine.

To make Vanilla Crème Fraîche, use the crème Chantilly recipe, but swap out the cream for crème fraîche, and hand-whisk to soft or medium peaks. This will split if you overwhisk it, and the only remedy is to start again with fresh ingredients.

Crème Pâtissière

This is a standard you must have in your repertoire. With it, you have a delicious, stable custard to fill choux buns, éclairs and mille-feuille, and slather between layers of cake, brioche or crepes. *So* much can be done with this, including adding interesting extracts and praline pastes to flavour the custard how you want. You can do this the old-fashioned way, in a non-stick pot over the stove, but in a microwave it just never goes wrong.

MAKES ABOUT 1.5 LITRES (52 FL OZ/6 CUPS)

INGREDIENTS

1 litre (35 fl oz/4 cups) milk

6 egg yolks + 2 extra whole eggs

200 g (7 oz) caster (superfine) sugar

100 g (3½ oz) wheaten cornflour (cornstarch), see note on page 33

60 g (2 oz) chilled unsalted butter, thinly sliced

2 teaspoons vanilla bean paste OR vanilla extract

1 tablespoon Cointreau OR Grand Marnier liqueur

METHOD

Microwave the milk in a large heatproof bowl for 4–5 minutes on the highest setting.

Meanwhile, whisk the egg yolks and extra eggs with the sugar until pale and thick. Do *not* allow the sugar to rest on the eggs for any length of time before whisking vigorously, or it will pickle the yolks unevenly and create a lumpy mixture. Whisk in the cornflour until smooth. Add to the hot milk, and whisk to combine.

Microwave for 2 minutes, then whisk madly until smooth. Repeat this twice, or until the mixture is very thick and swirls stay put like whipped cream. Cool for about 5 minutes, before whisking in the butter and vanilla until combined. Allow to cool for about 30 minutes, whisking enthusiastically every 10 minutes to get rid of any steam trapped in the custard and helping it to set. Cover with plastic wrap pressed directly onto the surface of the custard, and refrigerate overnight or until completely chilled before using. When ready to use, whip together the crème pâtissière and Cointreau with an electric mixer on high speed until silky and glossy.

If you want the crème pâtissière to be lighter, whisk in some Crème Chantilly (see page 203) or even a tiny bit of milk.

Yoghurt Mascarpone Cream

I love the look of surprise on people's faces when I give them a spoonful of this. They expect 'rich' and they expect 'cream', but what's wonderful is that, instead, they get this light, mildly sharp, vanilla-y, subtly sweet cultured flavour that, to be honest, trumps a conventional crème Chantilly in most cases. It doesn't always hold well, depending on what brands of yoghurt and mascarpone you use, so it's not good for engineering anything that needs to be structurally sound such as between layers of cake. It's best for dolloping generously on things like pavlova or other meringue desserts, slices of tea cake or poached fruit.

MAKES ABOUT 500 ML (17 FL OZ/2 CUPS)

INGREDIENTS

250 g (9 oz/1 cup) mascarpone cheese
250 g (9 oz/1 cup) Greek-style yoghurt
50 g (1¾ oz) icing (confectioners') sugar mixture
1–2 teaspoons vanilla bean paste OR vanilla extract

METHOD

Combine all the ingredients in a medium mixing bowl, and whisk until smooth. This will keep perfectly for up to 2 weeks in the fridge, seeing as both the cheese and the yoghurt are cultured forms of dairy.

Rum Custard

This is definitely another basic you need in your dessert armament because a warm veil of custard will cover a myriad of sins. Churn it, and magically it transforms into ice cream. You see how *need* is not an *exaggeration*? As with a crème pâtissière, you can make this using a good ol' pot on the stove, but the margin between success and disaster is drastically reduced if you employ the mod-con microwave. Oh, the insistence in most custard-making methodology of having to whisk like mad whilst slowly pouring the hot cream into the egg mixture is an urban myth; once the yolks are whisked with sugar, they are 'blanched' and hence stable. In the case of crème pâtissière, this is even more so because of the added cornflour. Emmanuel Mollois taught me that!

MAKES ABOUT 625 ML (21½ FL OZ/2½ CUPS)

INGREDIENTS

500 ml (17 fl oz/2 cups) thin (pouring) OR thickened (whipping) cream

6 egg yolks

50 g (1¾ oz/scant ¼ cup) caster (superfine) sugar

1 teaspoon vanilla bean paste OR vanilla extract OR vanilla essence

60 ml (2 fl oz/¼ cup) rum (brandy, Cointreau and Frangelico liqueur are good alternatives)

METHOD

Microwave the cream in a medium heatproof bowl for about 3 minutes on the highest setting. In a medium mixing bowl, whisk the egg yolks, sugar and vanilla until pale and thick, then pour into the hot cream. Whisk well, then microwave for 2 minutes. Whisk well once more, repeating this process until the custard thickens enough to easily coat the back of a wooden spoon without running off immediately.

Add the rum and stir to combine. If you want to turn this into ice cream, chill completely (overnight is best), then churn with an ice-cream maker following the manufacturer's instructions.

If you are worried you've overdone it and it looks like it's splitting, immediately bung it all into a blender, whizz it for a few seconds and it should come together. If not, then you've really murdered the thing and can either eat it regardless, seeing as it'll still be yummy, albeit with a slightly dodgy texture, or start again from scratch.

NOTE

When making any kind of custard, you must immediately and quickly whisk the yolks or whole eggs and sugar as soon as they are combined. If not, the sugar 'pickles' the yolks unevenly, which will result in a lumpy custard.

Shannon's Lemon Curd

This is my favourite lemon curd recipe, stolen from my friend and Jamface colleague Shannon, and I swear by it. It holds beautifully on tarts and gives just the right amount of citrus kapow to pancakes, pastries, cakes and maybe even toast on a naughty day.

MAKES ABOUT 750 ML (26 FL OZ/3 CUPS)

INGREDIENTS

Finely grated zest of 2–3 lemons
185 ml (6 fl oz/¾ cup) lemon juice
150 g (5½ oz/¾ cup) caster
    (superfine) sugar
125 g (4½ oz) butter, cut into
    2 cm (¾ inch) dice
5 eggs, whisked

METHOD

To make the curd, combine the zest, lemon juice and sugar in a large heatproof bowl, and whisk until combined.

Microwave for about 2 minutes on the highest setting, then whisk in the butter until melted. Buzz for another 2 minutes, add the eggs and whisk until well combined. Continue to buzz in 2-minute bursts at a time, whisking well in between, until luscious and thick.

If you are worried you've overdone it and it looks like it's splitting, immediately bung it all into a blender, whizz it for a few seconds and it should come together. If not, you can eat it regardless, albeit with a slightly dodgy texture, or start again from scratch. This keeps well in an airtight container in the fridge for up to 2 weeks.

Pâte Sablée, Two Ways

I absolutely swear by these two pâte sablée recipes. One thing that totally does my head in with making pastry is shrinkage. Often after blind-baking, your tart has wonky edges and has shrunk by half, and you are left with so little room for the filling it makes you want to tear your hair out. With this recipe, your pastry shells are rich, crisp and delicious, and come out looking identical to the way they went into the oven! Just watch you don't overhandle or let the pastry wilt, or it will become very hard to handle. If this happens, just pop it back into the fridge to stiffen up again. Regardless, the other magical quality this pastry has is that cracks and holes are easily patched and seal up on baking.

MAKES ABOUT 850 G (1 LB 14 OZ) PASTRY

CHOCOLATE PÂTE SABLÉE
180 g (6 oz) caster (superfine) sugar
100 g (3½ oz/1 cup) almond meal
260 g (9¼ oz 1¾ cups) plain (all-purpose) flour
½ teaspoon salt
55 g (2 oz/½ cup) Dutch process cocoa powder
200 g (7 oz) chilled unsalted butter, cut into 2 cm (¾ inch) dice
1 small egg

CHOCOLATE PÂTE SABLÉE
Pulse the sugar, almond meal, flour, salt and cocoa in a food processor until combined. Add the butter, and pulse until sandy. Add the egg, and process until the mixture begins to bind into a ball. Tip onto a clean work surface, and pat into a thick disc. Cover in plastic wrap, and refrigerate for 30 minutes.

ALMOND PÂTE SABLÉE
180 g (6 oz) caster (superfine) sugar
100 g (3½ oz/1 cup) almond meal
260 g (9¼ oz/1¾ cups) plain (all-purpose) flour
⅛ teaspoon salt
Finely grated zest of 1 orange
200 g (7 oz) chilled unsalted butter, cut into 2 cm (¾ inch) dice
1 small egg

ALMOND PÂTE SABLÉE
Pulse the sugar, almond meal, flour, salt and orange zest in a food processor until combined. Add the butter, and pulse until sandy. Add the egg, and process until the mixture begins to bind into a ball. Tip onto a clean work surface, and pat into a thick disc. Cover in plastic wrap, and refrigerate for 30 minutes.

Italian Meringue

This is the most stable of all the meringues. It's the best one to torch and for anything where you need the meringue to hold for long periods of time without going weird (splitting, collapsing) on you. This unique characteristic is achieved when boiling-hot sugar syrup is whisked into the egg whites at high speed and essentially blanches (or cooks) and stabilises them.

MAKES ABOUT 400 G (14 OZ) MERINGUE

INGREDIENTS

130–140 g (4¾–5 oz) egg whites (about 4 large)
200 g (7 oz) caster (superfine) sugar + 1 scant heaped tablespoon
100 ml (3½ fl oz) water

METHOD

Using an electric stand mixer, whisk the egg whites on high speed until medium peaks form. Add the extra tablespoon of sugar, and whisk until stiff peaks form, then turn off the machine.

Meanwhile, using a clean metal spoon, mix the 200 g (7 oz) of sugar and water in a small saucepan and bring to the boil, then leave it alone.

Hereon, my method for making this is unorthodox in that I don't use a thermometer because I don't like them. I go by sight, sound and smell. If you do want to use one, the temperature you want to reach is 118°–125°C (244°–257°F). Otherwise, just boil the sugar until you can see no more steam rising from the mixture.

The smell of the sugar will become richer. Immediately remove the saucepan from the heat. Quickly turn the mixer back on the highest speed and begin to drizzle a thread of the hot sugar syrup into the meringue. Be careful the whisk doesn't spray the sugar towards you here. Keep pouring patiently until all the sugar has been used, then reduce to the lowest speed and whisk for another 10–15 minutes until the bowl is cool to the touch.

Transfer the meringue to a piping bag and use immediately, or refrigerate it overnight to use the next morning.

big thanks & hugs to ...

Mum, for your perfectionism. Without it, I would never have learnt that attention to detail is everything. I'm sure the stoic team behind this book at Murdoch are cursing you for it but without it, this book would never have come to fruition. Truly everything I know about baking I inherited from watching you stubbornly cook things over and over until they were sensational, since I was yay high.

To Koo Poh, you've given our family the greatest gift possible, your selflessness, humility and want for nothing except to see us flourish as human beings. You taught me how to feel my way with ingredients, to taste unusual things and to be able to find beauty in the simplest of flavours.

Dad, my roller shutter-selling superman, for always encouraging me to dream big and live a creative life. Your enthusiastic support is often embarrassing but secretly appreciated.

My big bro, Casper, and his tribe, Teena, Trent, Tyler, Trini and Hayley, for your continual patience and understanding of the strange and wonky roads I choose to travel, which have me perpetually missing in action as a sister and aunty. I hope you all know I care about you deeply.

To my closest confidantes and Jamface compadres, Matt, Sarah and Gingy – for sharing all my miseries and happinesses whether you want to or not; Sarah for putting up with the weekly 'gate' scandals; Matt for all the early morning wig outs ... we will get there and breathe life into Bonaparte, and the Mighty Misfits and ALL the things. I promise!

Of course to my beautiful Joffy, who still thinks I'm wonderful even when I wake up looking like Medusa. Thank you for keeping me grounded, yet allowing me to be an utter nutter.

Rhino and Tim, without you guys there would be so many more melt downs. Thank you for looking ridiculous always and giving me so many laughs.

To my Jamface family, I feel very lucky to have a team of such whacky, amazing people to help realise our small biz dreams.

To my friend, Emmanuel, I wish so much you could have seen Jamface. Thank you for sharing everything you knew and loved about pastry with me. Without your encouragement and influence, Jamface and this book might never have happened. Forever when I think of you now, I will laugh and cry ... there were so many funny, joyful moments. May you rest in peace.

Finally, to the long-suffering team behind this book at Murdoch Books: Jane, Katie, Vivien, Siobhan and Sarah. Thank you for letting this book be completely me. We got there in the end and it's a beauty!

To Alan 'Squarepants' Benson and Michelle 'Nori' Noerianto for the stunning images, so many bad puns and those sublime 11pm finishes. I have one word for you both – H.U.R.R.Y!

index

**MADELEINES WITH STRAWBERRY
ROSEWATER GLAZE (page 34)**

BLUEBERRY BAKEWELL TART (page 93)

Published in 2017 by Murdoch Books, an imprint of Allen & Unwin

Murdoch Books Australia
83 Alexander Street
Crows Nest NSW 2065
Phone: +61 (0) 2 8425 0100
Fax: +61 (0) 2 9906 2218
murdochbooks.com.au
info@murdochbooks.com.au

Murdoch Books UK
Ormond House
26–27 Boswell Street
London WC1N 3JZ
Phone: +44 (0) 20 8785 5995
murdochbooks.co.uk
info@murdochbooks.co.uk

For Corporate Orders & Custom Publishing, contact
our Business Development Team at
salesenquiries@murdochbooks.com.au.

Publisher: Jane Morrow
Editorial Manager: Katie Bosher
Design Manager: Vivien Valk
Project Editor: Siobhan O'Connor
Designer: Sarah Odgers
Photographer: Alan Benson
Stylist: Michelle Noerianto
Production Manager: Lou Playfair

A cataloguing-in-publication entry is available
from the catalogue of the National Library of
Australia at nla.gov.au.

ISBN 978 1 74336 626 4 Australia
ISBN 978 1 74336 749 0 UK

A catalogue record for this book is available from
the British Library.

Colour reproduction by Splitting Image Colour
Studio Pty Ltd, Clayton, Victoria
Printed by C & C Offset Printing Co. Ltd., China

Murdoch Books wishes to thank Rock N Rustic
in Maylands, South Australia, for their help
sourcing props for the photo shoot.

IMPORTANT: Those who might be at risk from
the effects of salmonella poisoning (the elderly,
pregnant women, young children and those
suffering from immune deficiency diseases)
should consult their doctor with any concerns
about eating raw eggs.

OVEN GUIDE: You may find cooking times
vary depending on the oven you are using. For
fan-forced ovens, as a general rule, set the oven
temperature to 20°C (70°F) lower than indicated
in the recipe.

MEASURES GUIDE: We have used 20 ml
(4 teaspoon) tablespoon measures. If you
are using a 15 ml (3 teaspoon) tablespoon
add an extra teaspoon of the ingredient
for each tablespoon specified.